T0193856

Gullible's Travels

Stories from a Naive and Innocent Childhood

By Me
(David Random)

authorHOUSE®

AuthorHouse™
1663 Liberty Drive
Bloomington, IN 47403
www.authorhouse.com
Phone: 1 (800) 839-8640

Published by AuthorHouse 08/29/2015

ISBN: 978-1-5049-3422-0 (sc)
ISBN: 978-1-5049-3423-7 (e)

Library of Congress Control Number: 2015914156

Print information available on the last page.

This book is printed on acid-free paper.

The Stories

Introduction

I wasn't always so suave and sophisticated. Okay, I'm still not. But on a scale of human characteristics, I have, for the most part, outgrown my gullible naiveté, passed through the geekdom of my late teens and early twenties, and have settled at a somewhat comfortable middle ground somewhere between mature and overly serious. Looking back at my childhood, it is quite remarkable that I have arrived at this point in my life relatively undaunted by the occurrences leading up to it.

The events and beliefs recounted in the stories you are about to read represent a period in my life that still feels close, though not in years. There remains a great familiarity with the ideas, impressions, and opinions of my childhood. The fact that I am able to laugh and poke fun at the little boy who used to be me should not be taken as a sign of disrespect or superiority. I am very much aware that who I am today is a direct result of his guidance. Were he to read these stories, I believe he would share in the laughter without being embarrassed or insulted. I know this to be the case because he was there when I wrote them. He has added his voice and his indelible memories to the accounts that follow. He is still very much alive.

His innocence is not so much in evidence these days, as it has been covered over by a thin veneer of what would appear to an outsider as self-confidence. But he is still felt, loved, and nurtured. I carry him with me always, and I wish to thank him for his generous contributions to this book.

I would also like to take this opportunity to convey a sincere message and my wish for his future. Though I have thought it on many occasions, my fear is that, left unsaid, it will not be taken to heart. So, it is with heartfelt gratitude and love for his childish innocence that I leave him with these few words:

Never grow up.

Gullible's Travels

When I was considerably younger than current cir-
cumstances find me, my older cousin, Jerry, convinced me
that the soft, brown filling that comprised the inside of Fig
Newtons was, in fact, earwax. This was not so much an
indication of his powers of persuasion as it was my extreme
gullibility as a four-year-old. Because he was my elder by a
considerable measure (he was nine), I took Jerry's words on
good authority and considered it highly likely that such was
the case. I thought it quite plausible that there existed in
some far-off cookie factory an assembly line of diligent
workers prying the depths of their inner ears with their
pinkies and flicking the accumulated residue into a giant
vat where other workers carefully spooned it into the hol-
lows of the awaiting beige sleeves.

I tell you this not only to demonstrate my boundless
naiveté, legendary though it was, but to illustrate the
unshakable persistence of many of my early beliefs. You see,
even after I discovered the truth about what goes into Fig
Newtons, it was my initial perception of them that lingered.
Whenever they were divvied out by my grandmother, I
would happily offer mine to Jerry, who always seemed

pleased to relieve me of my share. To this day, though I am still fond of my cousin, my distaste for Fig Newtons remains entirely undiminished.

Many of the dubious claims that passed for truth in my childhood have never been completely discredited to my satisfaction as an adult, despite a somewhat more skeptical viewpoint. A lingering belief remains where there still exists even the remote possibility of truth. Until reliable scientific studies prove conclusively that toads do not give you warts, I'm not picking one up. I've also been told that dangling the hand of a sleeping person in warm water will cause him to wet the bed, though opportunities to verify this have proved to be rather elusive. And part of me still wants to believe that entire colonies of lemmings commit suicide by throwing themselves into the sea despite the nature shows on TV citing evidence to the contrary. It seems the more illogical or bizarre a claim, the more it must have some basis in truth, and therefore, should not be dismissed out of hand.

Growing up, I was able to discredit a variety of questionable claims either on my own or with the help of friends, but only as a result of careful observation or experimentation. Like the assertion that placing a penny on railroad tracks would result in a paper-thin copper wafer. I had little trouble accepting the fact that the shape of a coin might be substantially altered under the weight of a two-hundred-ton locomotive, though even this I would have to see with my own eyes. It was the attendant consequence of which I was not completely convinced. David Locke, a know-it-all schoolmate, had told me that doing so would result in the derailment of the entire train, an accomplishment for which I would, no doubt, be severely reprimanded. I pondered this possibility for several weeks before getting up the nerve to tempt fate and risk the outcome. I had heard stories about Peter McLeod, an older boy in the sixth grade, who had flattened a penny with apparently no negative consequences, and whose actions had yielded a nice, shiny medallion, though I had not actually seen the evidence for myself.

The day on which I decided to desecrate a penny, I waited while two silver passenger trains full of commuters sped past. If I was going to derail a train, I wanted to make certain that hundreds of lives would not be taken in the process. I would wait for a long and heavy freight train, so that the only lives lost would be those of the engineer and perhaps one or two crew members. After sitting in the coal yard for about forty minutes clutching a penny in my sweaty palm, I heard the faint, but distinct rumble of an approaching freight train. It was still one or two minutes away, and I slowly made my way out to where two sets of tracks passed between a large mill on one side and the backyards of a row of small clapboard houses on the other. I squatted down and placed a hand first on one set of tracks, and then the other. I had been told that feeling the vibrations coming through the steel rails was a reliable method of determining on which track the train would arrive. Detecting not the slightest sensation, (and apparently dispelling yet another rumor) I lingered long enough to make a visual sighting of the big locomotive as it slowly leaned around a bend in the track about a quarter mile to the west. A dog barked from behind a chain-link fence across the tracks as I carefully positioned my one-cent piece squarely on the appropriate rail. I rotated the coin so Mr. Lincoln's face looked confidently in the direction of the oncoming train, and ran back to the coal yard to hide behind a wooden barrier. There I would wait for what I hoped would not be a spectacular derailment.

The ground shook as the huge train approached and rumbled past with no consequence whatsoever. First, the giant locomotive. Then another, back to back, right behind the first. Then a succession of huge, brick-colored boxcars with large painted letters on the sides spelling out names like Burlington Northern, Santa Fe, and Southern. I felt a little silly that I had made such a big deal of what amounted to nothing at all. Peering through a crack in the barrier, I watched the long steel tracks move up and down under the enormous weight of each passing boxcar. How could I have believed David Locke's assertion that something as tiny as a penny could possibly have any effect on a huge locomotive? It was like expecting my dad's car to careen out of control because a bug hit the windshield. Now I was about to collect my reward. A token of my bravery and tangible proof that David Locke was wrong.

Minutes passed and still the endless chain of boxcars kept rumbling by. From my hiding place, I tried to spot the location of my penny, but could not determine exactly where I had placed it. Finally, the last of the long procession of cars had passed me, and I stood up and waved to the man in the caboose, feeling some relief that his life had been spared. As the sound of the train grew more distant, I headed for the tracks and stumbled across the raised bed of crushed stone to the spot where I hoped to collect my newly formed copper token. I searched for several minutes, moving the stones about with my feet. By now, the sound of the train had completely disappeared and all that remained was the incessant barking of the dog on the opposite side of the tracks. Certain that the coin had not simply vaporized, I searched a gradually widening area until, convinced that my search had now further hidden the coin among the stones, I accepted my loss, richer in the knowledge that it costs more than a penny to derail a freight train.

Over time, my friends and I saw one belief after another revealed as fallacy. One by one, a succession of dubious claims were exposed as having been wildly exaggerated. I was often embarrassed that I had at one time accepted such hyperbole as fact. Some former beliefs now seem laughable in hindsight. Like the suggestion that you could blow up a car by jamming a potato into its exhaust pipe. And the belief that if you swam within an hour after eating, you'd get cramps and drown. Or that a cherry bomb flushed down a toilet in the boys room would cause all the other toilets to erupt, causing severe plumbing damage. Okay, that one actually turned out to be true. The point is that much of what I had accepted as fact had absolutely no basis in truth.

The whole Santa Claus thing notwithstanding, my entire childhood was characterized by an eager and enthusiastic acceptance of outlandish hearsay, deliberately deceptive claims, and assorted urban legends. The erroneous statements of misinformed friends were allowed to go unquestioned. In fact, the more outlandish a claim, the more I was prone to believe it. It was far more exciting to believe in the remote possibility of something that was really astonishing. To dismiss a claim merely because its credibility was suspect would close the door to a whole world of wonder and awe that, as an elementary school student, I thrived on.

On the last page of nearly every issue of Archie comic books was a claim that, if true, would be the most amazing, the most astounding phenomenon I could imagine. It was the king of all claims. And there it was printed right in black and white. In a publication created by adults and sold in stores all across America. Surely it must be true. And surely it would be worth the one dollar I would have to surrender to find out. The whole page, in fact, was filled with compelling merchandise from a company called Honor House. Even their name suggested that my faith in their claims was certainly not unwarranted.

One item was a device you put into your mouth that enabled you to throw your voice, or so the ad stated, into trunks and behind doors. It came with a free book on how to use it to fool friends, family, and teachers. That item was only twenty-five cents. There was also a device called a moneymaker in which you could turn a plain piece of paper into a real one dollar bill. The illustration showed a grown man smiling as he apparently demonstrated the phenomenon. But it got better. Take the one dollar bill and reinsert it into the same device and a five dollar bill would emerge. The five could then be turned into a ten. This item cost one dollar and twenty-five cents. But even at eight years old, the effectiveness of such a device seemed highly suspect to me. If the gadget actually worked, it wouldn't be such a secret, and I'm certain my dad would have purchased one so as not to have missed out on the opportunity to buy me more toys with

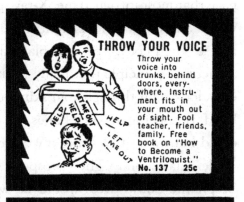

THROW YOUR VOICE
Throw your voice into trunks, behind doors, everywhere. Instrument fits in your mouth out of sight. Fool teacher, friends, family. Free book on "How to Become a Ventriloquist." No. 137   25c

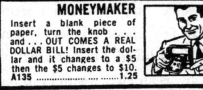

MONEYMAKER
Insert a blank piece of paper, turn the knob . . . and . . . OUT COMES A REAL DOLLAR BILL! Insert the dollar and it changes to a $5 then the $5 changes to $10. A135 ....1.25

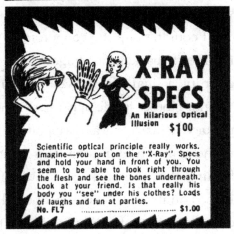

X-RAY SPECS
An Hilarious Optical Illusion $1 00

Scientific optical principle really works. Imagine—you put on the "X-Ray" Specs and hold your hand in front of you. You seem to be able to look right through the flesh and see the bones underneath. Look at your friend. Is that really his body you "see" under his clothes? Loads of laughs and fun at parties.
No. FL7   .... $1.00

his newfound wealth.

Other featured merchandise included a whoopie cushion, onion-flavored chewing gum, smoke bombs, and a trick
baseball. But this was all kids' stuff whose novelty would, no
doubt, wear off quickly. It was the item at the bottom of the
page that most intrigued me. X-ray specs, the ad insinuated,
would allow you to look right through someone's clothing
and see their body. The ad explained that this was based on
a scientific principle that really worked, and said you could
even look right through your skin and see the bones in your
hand. But seeing my own bones was not what excited me. I
could hardly wait to bring my X-ray specs into my third-
grade classroom. The prospect of looking through
Stephanie Lord's dress would be well worth four weeks'
allowance. Stephanie was a petite, soft-spoken classmate
who had the cutest dimples I had ever seen. She was also my
girlfriend, though I hadn't exactly told her yet. I was much
too shy as an eight-year-old to have approached her with
such a forward declaration.

I couldn't clip the coupon fast enough. But the wait for
my return package was agonizing. After what seemed an
eternity, a small, flat envelope arrived bearing the words
"Honor House" in the upper left corner. Having anticipated a
package to arrive, I was disappointed to see only an envelope
in the mail. Thinking that this must be a notification con-
firming that the package containing my X-ray specs was
indeed on its way, I carefully opened the envelope. I unfolded a thin piece of cardboard in the shape of eyeglasses, the

lenses of which consisted of two pieces of colored cellophane, one red, and one green. Holding them up to my face, everything appeared to have a double image. A kind of multi-colored outline that made objects look... well, kind of like the comics page of the Sunday paper when the different colored inks are printed out of register.

This time my gullibility meter was off the charts. It had cost me a whole dollar. And if that wasn't bad enough, Honor House had added insult to injury by charging me another fifteen cents to cover shipping and handling. My X-ray specs eventually found their way to the back of my desk drawer where they remained as an occasional reminder of my willingness to accept any lie that was stated with enough conviction. To my knowledge, Stephanie Lord was never aware of the desperate crush I had on her or of my secret plan to render her clothing transparent.

But that was a long time ago. I have outgrown my tendencies toward childish gullibility. No longer am I taken in by preposterous claims that defy all logic with the alluring promise of amazing payoffs in exchange for a dollar and some change. Today, my gullibility has taken on epic proportions with far more serious consequence than the loss of a mere week's allowance or the ridicule of adolescent schoolmates. The gullibility of my adulthood has been extravagantly exemplified by substantial deficits to my savings account as well as my ego. X-ray specs have been replaced by hot stock tips. Far-fetched urban legends like

Mikey of Life cereal fame who, it is rumored, died when his stomach exploded as a result of swallowing Pop Rocks candy with Coca-Cola, are now overshadowed by my belief in political candidates' promises of peace and prosperity in exchange for my vote. A quotation pinned to my parents' bulletin board seems to have been placed there for my benefit, though they have repeatedly denied a deliberate connection. It states simply, "Keep an open mind. But don't let your brains fall out." As an adult, the desire to believe often seems to occupy a more prominent place in my brain than does the concept of logic, and I have been presented with innumerable opportunities to demonstrate this imbalance.

It seemed considerably far-fetched, for example, that in 1960, aliens had landed right here in my current home state of New Hampshire. It seemed even more unlikely that Betty Hill, the woman now sitting right in my parents' living room, had not only witnessed the entire episode but, in fact, had been abducted, along with her husband, Barney, taken aboard the UFO, and subjected to extensive physical examination.

But here she was sitting on my parents' sofa recounting the event without sensationalism, as if it were a trip to the grocery store. She was a sweet lady with an honest face. And I believed her story. What's more, I believed that *she* believed her story. Had my only knowledge of this astonishing claim come as a result of reading the account in some book, I might have attributed the motive to publicity or greed, and read it, at least in part, as science fiction. (In fact, a book about the incident, *The Interrupted Journey* by John Fuller, was published by Dial Press in 1966, a fact that now seemed only to reinforce the credibility of Betty's bizarre story.)

When we questioned her about the experience, she answered with conviction but without drama. Not wanting to openly display my tendency toward belief in the unbelievable, I closed my gaping mouth and listened with wide-eyed, but polite dispassion. The possibility that this extraordinary event might have actually happened, however, overran my skepticism, as there seemed to be considerable evidence to substantiate her story. It was all in the book. The one piece of information I wanted to know, however, concerned the physical examinations that the aliens had performed on Betty and Barney. How was it possible that the aliens had peered inside the bodies of their captives while leaving no visible scars as evidence? That information was missing from the book, and Betty had not elaborated. Ultimately, I decided not to ask my burning question. And now that both Betty and Barney have passed away, I fear I will forever be forced to rely on my own logic and supposition for the answer. It now seems quite clear to me that there could be only one plausible explanation. The aliens must have used X-ray specs.

A Legend in My Own Mind

At twelve, I was a skinny kid with eyeglasses and braces on my teeth. I also had selective vision. This is the only thing that could possibly account for the fact that I had convinced myself that the reflection looking back at me in the mirror bore a distinct and striking resemblance to heart-throb Ricky Nelson.

Knowing in my heart that other people saw me more as a Howdy Doody type did not stop me, however, from attempting to comb my hair in such a way as to emulate the rock star. I was certain that with a little work, and a lot of Brylcreem, my hair alone might allow others to see the uncanny resemblance. My hair, however, remained defiantly averse to doing what it was not naturally prone to do. It curled where I wanted it to be straight, and flipped where I wanted it only to wave.

Ultimately, I had to come to terms with the fact that I would always have Bobby Vinton's hair. Kind of curly, kind of frizzy, and decidedly uncool. Of course, Bobby Vinton could get away with it because he could sing. He had the advantage of getting girls to fall in love with him on the radio before they knew what his hair looked like.

Then in the early sixties, as music evolved, folk singers started to become more popular. Folk singers didn't use grease in their hair or force it into exaggerated and cartooney sculptures. For the most part, folk singers kept their hair natural, although the popular ones all had silky smooth and straight hair that cascaded down over one side of their foreheads like pages tumbling from a loosely bound book. It did this naturally without having to be manipulated. When they sang, they casually flipped their heads back between verses and a gentle sweep of bangs would flip out of their eyes until they once again looked down at their guitars. Then the whole head-flip process would start again.

But the folk singer hairstyle suited me no better than the rock star look. My hair was not of a naturally silky texture, a fact about which I was in denial until I began growing my hair longer, and my friends started calling me Brillo. I tried to perfect the head-flipping gesture, but found that my hair did not actually move, and people just thought I had a nervous tic.

For a time, I thought I had licked the problem and took to plastering my hair down at night with a sticky, blue setting gel called Dippity-Doo, brushing it straight and going to bed wearing a stocking cap on my head. This worked reasonably well most of the time, and by morning, my hair was remarkably straight, although so flat that from a distance it appeared to be only painted on my scalp. It also meant that I could not touch my hair all day or get it wet. If it was rainy or breezy, my hair would take off in all directions like a pile of dead leaves scattering in the wind. Once in a while, the stocking cap I wore to bed would shift during the night and I would be forced to go to school with what looked like a chicken wing protruding from the side of my head.

Of course, my mother would tell you that I was handsome beyond belief. I would venture to say that her biased assessment of my appearance was the only thing that was beyond belief.

The day I finally got my braces off was a momentous occasion that I had looked forward to with eager anticipation. I had become used to seeing the metallic scaffolding and gridwork that, for two years, had covered more than half the surface area of my teeth, and I had forgotten that there were actually whole teeth hiding somewhere beneath it all waiting to make their grand reappearance. For all of twenty-four months, I had dreamed about how I would look with a perfect, straight smile, and imagined I would now even more closely resemble Frankie Avalon and that guy, Bobby, from *The Lawrence Welk Show*. When the orthodontist finally removed the last of my braces, and scrubbed my teeth clean, he proudly handed me a hand mirror and, without saying a word, waited for me to react. This would be the first time in many months that I would be able to actually see the whole surface of my teeth, rather than just bits of them peeking out around the elaborate metal hardware.

I'm not certain that I did a very good job of hiding my

initial shock. For what was instantly and glaringly obvious was not how straight my teeth were, but how huge they were. My God, they were enormous! I looked like I had a mouthful of perfectly aligned piano keys. Sliding my tongue over what seemed like an acre of highly polished, unobstructed tile flooring, I was sure that the first thing people would notice about me was not how much I now looked like Frankie Avalon, but how closely I resembled Mr. Ed.

It took about a week of staring at myself in the bathroom mirror, but gradually my teeth reverted to the size I had remembered them to be before being encased in tiny suits of armor. Over time, I grew less self-conscious of my gigantic, naked teeth, and came to realize that I actually had quite a pleasant smile. But these eyeglasses have got to go.

I had resigned myself to the fact that frames and lenses would always be part of the familiar landscape of my face and that I would forever view the world through little panes of glass. The world would always see them as part of who I was. The frames changed occasionally over the years as I outgrew or broke them, but they were never very stylish, and I had always secretly wished that I didn't have to wear them at all.

My first pair of eyeglasses came about, ironically, because I couldn't hear. I was in the second grade when my entire class was marched down to the nurse's office to line up and have our vision checked. Being arranged in alphabetical order, I was near the back of the line when the nurse gave us our instructions. When each student reached the front of the line, we were to put our face up to a giant contraption that looked like one of those telescope things they put at scenic vistas that you put a quarter into in order to see distant mountains up close. (I got to do that once when my grandmother splurged and paid for thirty seconds of telescope time that my sister and I had to share. I didn't tell her that you could see the mountains better when you didn't have to squint through that huge machine. And besides, the eyeholes were too far apart to look through with both eyes at once.) The nurse who was administering the vision test continued her instructions and said something about holding our hand up and pointing at something. That's the part I couldn't hear.

But I had carefully watched each kid in front of me go through a curious series of hand gestures, holding up three fingers at a time, and alternating the direction in which they pointed. Up, down, left, right, and so forth. When my turn finally came, I pushed my face up against the big telescope with my eyes positioned at the two little eyeholes. I was happy to see that I could look through both holes at the same time. There were no pictures of mountains, however. Just rows of what looked like the letter "E" all facing in different directions. Some were correct, but others were lying on their backs or facing backward. I was too shy to ask the nurse to repeat the instructions, so I confidently mimicked the random series of hand gestures like my classmates before me had done. It was fun. Needless to say, however, for having set the school record for the most incorrect answers, I flunked the eye exam with enthusiastic aplomb. As luck would have it, it turned out I needed glasses anyway.

After I had been wearing glasses for about five years, and had become used to being called "four eyes," something unexpected happened that really opened my eyes. A rock 'n roll singer named Buddy Holly started making hit records and became very popular, especially with the girls. I was surprised when I saw his picture on the cover of his sheet music to see that he wore glasses. But not just any glasses. Big, heavy, black-framed glasses that encircled his eyes as if someone had taken a thick black marker and defaced his picture. When I saw him on The Ed Sullivan Show, he looked kind of goofy and awkward. They showed a close-up of his face that made his glasses look really big. All the girls in the audience screamed and didn't seem to mind at all that he wore glasses. It was the first time I ever thought that having eyeglasses might actually be kind of cool, and I petitioned my parents for new glasses with thick, heavy frames.

I thought perhaps at last this was my big break. Not only did Buddy Holly wear huge eyeglasses, but he was skinny with a kind of curly, misbehaving hair. And he had big teeth, too. If this were to become a widespread trend, I'd certainly fit right into this new look. But my hopes died when Buddy Holly's plane crashed in 1959, killing him prematurely, and with him, my one chance to finally be in style. No one stepped up to continue the nerdy-cool trend.

Stardom sought out only those with the natural good looks of those who had come before him. And with that, things went back to the way they had always been. And I went off to junior high school.

For a while, I tried not wearing my glasses. I needed them to read, but found I could walk quite adequately without them and without bumping into things or ending up in the girls' room by mistake. My senior photo that appears in my high school yearbook is without eyeglasses, and shows me with frizzy hair and big teeth squinting out from the pages where classmates who were voted "most popular" and "most likely to succeed" all had the natural good looks that would undoubtedly justify their titles.

Another tactic I attempted to employ was to hang around with the most nerdy kids in school, thinking that I might look good by comparison. I befriended geeky-looking kids with acne who were always the last ones picked for the volleyball teams in phys ed. Harry Peter's acne, in fact, was so bad that other students called him Harry Pizza. I also hung around with a guy whose nickname was Dribble. The kid, I swear, had no chin. From his lower lip, his face sloped directly down to his neck. I don't know how he ever learned to put on a pillow case. At any rate, I found that this comparison tactic did not work. When you see a group of kids walking down the corridor who look like they're going to a meeting of the algebra club, your first thought isn't, "Hey, that one kid looks pretty cool compared to the others."

It also didn't help that as we all started getting our

driver's licenses, some friends got to drive their families' shiny, late-model sedans or a little sports car belonging to their father, while I, on the other hand, usually rode my bike everywhere and felt fortunate when I was able to occasionally take sole command of my family's used Chevrolet station wagon. Even the overweight Walter Lucas, who caused his parents' brand new Impala convertible to list slightly toward the driver's side whenever he sat there, often had a girl sitting beside him in the passenger seat.

I may not have been the most popular kid in school. I was pretty quiet and shy. But I had my small circle of friends consisting mostly of others whose presence was nearly invisible to all but each other. We were not the athletes, class officers, or even the class cut-ups. But I was good at those solitary activities like art and music, and was basically happy. I was content to let others receive the accolades of fellow students and the trophies from their coaches.

So, believe me when I tell you that no one was more surprised than I was when I began playing my electric guitar and singing at parties and high school dances, and found that people crowded around me and applauded. Girls started coming up to me afterward and talking. Popular girls who usually hung out only with jocks like Chip Putnam all of a sudden were asking me questions like, "Is it hard to play the guitar?" and "Can you teach me to play?" Once, two cheerleaders came up to me and kissed me on both cheeks at the same time, leaving behind reddish lipstick smears that I did not notice until after I had stopped blushing. I didn't wash my face for two days.

Now all of a sudden, I was kind of glad I wasn't just

 another jock. It was okay that I didn't blend in with the kids whose popularity was only the result of their generic good looks. I was finally beginning to realize it wasn't so bad being me—a skinny, nerdy kid with glasses.

Move over, Chip. Buddy Holly is back.

My Unexpectedly Short Career as an Acrobat

*K*ids are experimenters. It's how we learn. It's how we decide that we don't like the taste of earthworms. It's how we figure out the difference between grasshoppers and wasps. It's how we determine that the stove burner is too hot to touch... again.

Kids are also pretenders. Child psychologists tell us that playing make-believe actually plays a real-life role in brain development by increasing cognitive and social skills as well as problem solving, goal setting, and confidence. This role-playing also expands our capacity for imagination. Playing house, playing doctor, and playing cowboys are all ways for us to increase the mental capabilities we will use as adults.

There was a time when my aspirations for what I would be "when I grow up" changed almost weekly. Alternately I wanted to be a cowboy, a rock 'n roll star, a major league baseball pitcher, and, owing to a shortlived fascination with bugs, an entomologist. Though I did not pursue the medical field, I must admit that playing doctor always held a certain fascination for me, although I was usually assigned the role of patient. It was from these early playtimes that I knew my friend, Dennis, was destined for success. Whenever we played doctor with neighborhood kids, he always wanted to be the lawyer.

Soon after my entomology phase, or maybe it was before, something happened that, for a very brief period, I thought was going to change my life. The Ringling Brothers Circus came to town, and my mother took my sister and me on the train all the way to Boston to be dazzled by the extravagant pageant. And dazzled I was. The astounding circus performers I saw were transfixing. They made it look so easy. One man in colorful tights, whom I took to be the leader of the acrobatic troupe, climbed to the top of a metal ladder, pausing periodically on his ascent to dramatically gesture to the crowd by extending one arm in a sweeping motion that I found very effective. It caused several audience members sitting in my vicinity to stop eating their popcorn and pay very close attention. When he arrived at the pinnacle of his climb, he hooked one leg around the top of the ladder and smiling, gestured with both arms outstretched at once. His expression then became suddenly more serious. The music that had been playing in the orchestra pit stopped and the crowd hushed appropriately, sensing that whatever was about to happen, was about to happen.

A drum roll further added to the tension as the man held both arms out in front of him as if he were about to do a swan dive into a swimming pool. But there was no pool.

Below him was what looked like a seesaw painted in bright circus designs and balancing at the middle on what appeared to be a large drum-shaped object resting on its side. On the far end of the seesaw stood another man whose weight caused the opposite end to extend upward at a steep angle toward the man on the ladder. Everyone knew what was going to happen. But seeing it would be something else entirely.

When he was quite certain that the anticipation of the crowd had reached its peak, the man at the top of the ladder confidently jumped from his lofty perch, landing on the high end of the seesaw, and subsequently launching the second man on a graceful trajectory onto the shoulders of yet another awaiting troupe member. This maneuver was repeated until three men stood balancing on each others' shoulders in a virtual tower of brightly colored, tight-wearing men. To the great appreciation and enthusiastic approval of the crowd, the human totem pole then disassembled itself by jumping one by one onto the seesaw, alternately flipping the previous man into a neatly formed line where they took their rehearsed and well-deserved bows.

It was at this moment that I envisioned my exciting future taking shape under bright spotlights accompanied by an orchestra wearing festive costumes, and complete with drums and a tuba. My gym teacher, Miss Stearns, had always made a special point of telling me how good I was at tumbling. And I was quite sure that I would be excellent at the sweeping arm gestures. On the way home on the train, clutching an armload of circus souvenirs, I thought to myself, "Okay, that's it. I'm going to be an acrobat."

It was subsequently brought to my attention by the older brother of a friend that making a living as an acrobat might prove to be even more challenging than the strength and agility needed to perform the necessary gymnastic feats. Employment opportunities for acrobats are even fewer than for cowboys, he noted. Even the largest companies in the world—General Motors, IBM, and even the government, he pointed out, employed virtually no acrobats.

That did not diminish my infatuation with the world of acrobatics, and I began my search for possible candidates to assist me in honing the necessary skills. I settled on Stevie Mason, a neighborhood kid perhaps three years my junior, and still light enough for me to successfully launch through the air in a series of twisting and arching somersaults. A scrawny kid with a blonde crew cut, Stevie was not entirely enamored with the idea at first, but repeated assurance of his safety (and the threat of being banned from our neighborhood clubhouse) eventually softened his reluctance. I told him, if we got good enough, we might even convince other local kids to come see us perform by paying an admission price of a nickel, a penny of which would go to Stevie.

*P*reparations for our feat of aerial mastery took the better part of two days. Everything had to be just right. As it happened, attached to the back of our small barn was a woodshed, the roof of which seemed a perfect height from which to initiate my leap down onto the upper reaches of the seesaw that I had fashioned from a long plank I had found in the shed. It seemed adequately sturdy, being about two inches thick, as wide as a schoolbook, and several times my height. I had tested its durability by supporting each end between two large concrete blocks and jumping repeatedly in the middle. Convinced of its strength, I went about the business of finding a suitable fulcrum on which to balance it. I found a small sawhorse in the barn which, although a bit high, certainly appeared to be stable enough.

I had jumped from the woodshed roof before and was not intimidated by its height. But never onto the leading edge of a seesaw. And never with the anticipation of such spectacular results. Still recalling the graceful image of the acrobats in tights, I explained to Stevie that he should not be frightened, and that the force of my jump would provide the necessary propulsion allowing him to land firmly on his feet, unaffected by his brief somersault through the air. Once again, I pictured the circus acrobats performing their fluid and graceful maneuver and imagined myself at the top of the tall ladder I had seen at the circus. Stevie trustingly stood at attention on the lower end of the big plank awaiting what can only be described in retrospect as neither fluid nor graceful.

The visual memory of what happened during the next three seconds is one of the most vivid and most disturbing of my entire childhood, and I struggle even now to find adequate words to convey its twisted and grotesque nature. It appeared to happen in slow motion. I sounded a mock drum roll before my feet left their perch at the edge of the roof. I was halfway to the seesaw when I realized I had forgotten to do my all-important arm movements. But it was too late. In a moment in which it became painfully clear that somehow everything had gone terribly wrong, I landed with the solid force of dead weight opposite my considerably lighter assistant.

Had I made a more thorough analysis of the performance I had witnessed at the circus, I might have concluded that, although my attention was on the man jumping from the ladder, the acrobat who was about to be flung aloft might have certain responsibilities in the process to ensure the completion, and thus, the success of the maneuver. It had not occurred to me until this very moment that some reaction might be required on his part—a jump, a flip, something to which the whiplike force of the seesaw would act as simply an added boost. I had not provided Stevie with any such instructions other than to stand perfectly still and wait to be dazzled.

The laws of physics being what they are, the resulting consequence could not have been otherwise. I landed directly across from Stevie, squarely facing him at the opposite end of the big plank, expecting to see him launched upward and out of my direct line of sight. I watched his legs and feet jolt upward with the snap of the board, but his hea... his head remained absolutely fixed in place as we stared directly into each other's eyes for what seemed an interminably long time. The upward slam of the rising plank had caused his legs to buckle and his skinny, limp body to fold under him like an accordion, compressing his spine in the process. I stood in silent shock, staring eye to eye with Stevie, surprised to find myself still directly facing him only armlengths away on opposite ends of the board, each waiting for the other to say or do something.

I didn't have to wait long. The silence lasted only a few seconds before Stevie started to bawl. Although he did appear to be several inches shorter than the height at which I was accustomed to seeing him, I was never so grateful for anything as the fact that he apparently was still able to walk. This he immediately demonstrated by running direct-ly home, still crying uncontrollably.

"Wait!" I called after him. "I forgot to do my arm move-ments." But Stevie could not hear my calls. He was halfway home by the time I realized I could be in big trouble and I had better hide the evidence before his father showed up. But his father did not show up. I did not see Stevie again until the next day while waiting for the school bus when, I swear to God, he had still not fully regained his normal height.

Stevie and I remained friends for the next few years, never discussing our brief attempt at gymnastic artistry. Stevie was subsequently granted full access to the club-house, and was allowed to partake in the modest refresh-ments we at times provided, even though he had not con-tributed to their purchase.

After several years, Stevie moved to the west coast with his parents where he, no doubt, helped in great measure to pay for some chiropractor's yacht. A mutual friend told me years later that, although barely five foot six, Stevie eventually became a highway patrolman in California. That was some years ago, and I have since lost touch with him, but when last I heard, Stevie was married and had at least two kids of his own. As far as I know, he is still a highway patrolman. I am still not an acrobat.

Getting Off on the Wrong Foot

"I hate dancing lessons!"

I don't remember if the sentiment was expressed aloud or if I just sulked silently in the back seat. We were on our way to the elementary school gymnasium where, on a weekly basis, my parents paid good money for me to hone my skills at complaining.

"They make us bow to the girls," I ranted, "and talk polite and everything. It's embarrassing."

"One day you'll be glad to have had the opportunity," they insisted, "to learn the finer points of ballroom artistry. Over the years, you'll be going to lots of weddings and other social functions. This will prevent you from embarrassing yourself by demonstrating your lack of social graces."

This was probably true. At the rate I was going, my embarrassment would undoubtedly be used up by then. I slouched in the back seat, anticipating another evening of drudgery while staring down at my feet and memorizing the steps required to execute a perfect box step. Step, step, slide. Step, step, slide.

My father pulled the car up to the side entrance of the

school and I grudgingly slid from the vinyl seat.

"I *hate* dancing lessons." This time I said it out loud, but I had already slammed the car door and my words rose unheard into the night air over the dark parking lot.

The school looked very different at night. Its darkened windows were a reminder that most other kids, indeed the rest of the free world, was home watching television. To make matters worse, Thursday was one of the best TV nights. *Zorro* was on. And while many of my friends were watching the masked horseman once again outwit the bumbling Sergeant Garcia, I, on the other hand, found myself reluctantly plodding toward the big double doors of the school. I trudged through the pool of fluorescent light that spilled out from the tiled hallway onto my newly polished shoes, and with a loud clang, I pushed open one side of the metal fire doors.

Once inside the school, my footsteps echoed down the deserted main corridor toward the first-floor gymnasium. The beige tile that paved the way was well worn, but highly polished. Mr. Tuttle, the janitor, was skilled at keeping the old wing of the McCarthy School looking clean, though it dated from the 1930s. No amount of disinfectant, however, could have masked the rancid smell of dirty sweat socks. It was a familiar smell that did not seem out of place in gym class, but now, dressed in my shirt and tie, it seemed suddenly offensive.

At the far end of the corridor I joined a small group of equally unenthusiastic fifth and sixth graders who had paused just short of the entrance in an attempt to delay the inevitable. Most of the boys looked uncomfortably out of place. Normally, we found plenty to laugh and joke about when we were playing baseball or throwing rocks into Old Man Campbell's pond. But tonight our impending fate had dampened our spirits to a hush. We stood, shifting uncomfortably from one foot to the other while self-consciously eyeing each others' unfamiliar wardrobes. It was clear from looking around that tying a necktie was a talent that would come only with practice. To boys who had taken weeks to master a few knots in the Boy Scout handbook, the subtle mechanics of such an elegant fashion accessory did not come easily.

One by one, additional stragglers shuffled down the corridor to join the growing huddle of adolescent boys. When enough boys had assembled for us to enter the gymnasium as a group without drawing too much individual attention, we took the final few steps together into the bright glare of the lights that hung overhead. Mr. Treyz was standing just inside the cavernous gym and greeted us as we entered. When he smiled, his rosy cheeks shone as if he had scrubbed and buffed them for the occasion. He welcomed everyone by name, occasionally adding the word "mister" or "miss" as if we shared his enthusiasm for such an adult pursuit.

By the time class began, a few more girls than boys had assembled. The boys gathered on one side of the hall and remained mute, resigned to our shared fate. The girls, in sharp contrast, were chatting and giggling on the opposite side of the room and did not seem to dread what was about to transpire. On the floor between us, the painted lines of the basketball court brought to mind the countless hours spent in this very same gym, running and yelling with wild excitement. Those times now seemed very distant. On command from Mr. Treyz, each group stood in a neat line in front of a row of folding chairs that faced each other on either side of the spacious room. Previous classes had determined our relative starting positions, and we obediently fell into place like two opposing armies awaiting the signal to attack.

Before the formalities would begin, however, Mr. Treyz walked to the middle of the floor for the mandatory and humiliating inspection. He gave a cursory nod to the girls' side of the room.

"You young ladies look very charming tonight," he proclaimed.

Then, approaching the lineup of boys, he had us hold our hands out in front of us, palms down, as he slowly made his way from one end to the other for the obligatory fingernail check, while explaining the importance of good hygiene. To his credit, I never heard him actually say that any of us had dirty fingernails, but once in a while he would take a boy's hands, turn them over, then look up at the boy with raised eyebrows. Words could not have added to the boy's already evident embarrassment. It always made me glad that I had remembered to wash my hands. Occasionally, he asked one of us to stand up straight,

explaining that good posture is fundamental to good dancing. But that was not as embarrassing as being caught with
dirty fingernails.

After inspection had taken up the first five minutes of
class, both rows of students were directed to sit down in the
chairs facing each other on opposite sides of the gymnasium. A quick count told me that several girls would find it
necessary to dance with each other as, typically, the girls
outnumbered the boys. I scanned the row of eager-looking
girls in an attempt to plan my strategy when the time came
for choosing a partner. Most of the girls I knew from school.
A few were familiar to me only by sight, but I had danced
with many during previous classes, and I knew whom to
avoid. Sheila Hammond always tried to lead, so I would
steer clear of that end of the row. And Connie Roberts wore
so much perfume that I found it difficult to dance and hold
my breath at the same time. There was really only one girl
I wanted to dance with.

Martha Parks was new to town and had joined the class
midway through the school year. I had wanted to dance
with her since the first week she arrived, but had never gotten the chance. I secretly watched her, and between lessons
wondered if she would be in class the following week. She
had a shy, sweet smile and silky blonde hair that poured
over her shoulders like honey. Though I'd never spoken to
her, and was quite sure she had not even noticed me, I
thought dancing with her might make Thursday evenings a
little less awful. I would need to plan my strategy carefully

though. I couldn't rush directly over to her. That would be too obvious. Besides, Mr. Treyz insisted that we walk like little gentlemen. And if someone else got to Martha first, I'd be afraid of showing my disappointment. But if I was too nonchalant in my approach, I'd be forced to settle for the leftovers. And no one wanted to dance with the leftovers. It was a delicate balance, and I would have to play it just right.

I was sure that other boys also wanted to dance with Martha because she was so pretty. But I tried not to look at her or appear too eager and tip my hand. The thought also occurred to me that if two of us reached her at the same time and Martha chose the other boy instead, I'd be mortified. *God, I hate dancing lessons!*

But before any choosing of partners took place, Mr. Treyz took center stage with his wife to demonstrate the fox trot. Mrs. Treyz never said a word during any of the dance classes. She let Mr. Treyz guide her around the floor while they both maintained an unnaturally stiff and upright posture. They were always in perfect step with each other, although they looked somewhat forced and uncomfortable. Almost mechanical. Mr. Treyz was careful to point out the correct position of the boy's right hand resting gently on the girl's left shoulder blade. This provided a buffer should the couple bump into other dancers while moving around the dance floor. I believe Mr. Treyz used the word "gliding" around the dance floor, but we all knew that gliding was beyond our present capabilities. For now, we would settle for just moving.

After the fox trot had been adequately demonstrated, Mr. Treyz bowed to his wife in an overly formal gesture that made it look as if they were attending a royal ball. He then returned to the front of the gym to lift the needle from the phonograph record. Before restarting the music, he invited the boys to choose partners.

"Gentlemen," he announced, "please select a young lady to be your partner."

As fifteen boys jostled for position crossing the floor, politely shoving and bumping as we went, Mr. Treyz added, "... and *walk!*" I would say the ground we had to cover was approximately the distance between home plate and first base. Some of the boys covered the span in little more time than it took to beat out an infield hit. I headed toward the end of the row where Martha Parks waited with her ankles crossed and her hands folded neatly in her lap. But halfway across the gymnasium, Dick Perkins cut right in front of me, causing me to alter my course. Then three other boys pushed in front of me, nudging me toward the middle of the row of girls. Suddenly, I found myself standing flat-footed directly in front of Linda Nichols. Before I could stop myself, I blurted out, "May I have this dance?"

Linda Nichols, or as she was known to many of us, "Olive Oyl," stood a good three inches taller than me and had the sharpest elbows on the east coast. Her jerky movements made it difficult to avoid stepping repeatedly on her gigantic feet, and though I tried desperately to glide, I was constantly reminded of the time my dad tried to show me how to operate the clutch in our old Ford. Whenever I started, she stopped. When I went left, she went right. Once, she bumped into me so hard that she knocked my glasses askew and I had to remove my hand from her bony shoulder blade to set them straight. It was torture. And for this I was missing *Zorro.*

The longest fox trot in history mercifully came to an end, and my injuries being minimal, I was able to escort Olive Oyl back to her seat and retreat to the relative safety of the boys' side of the room. Mr. Treyz once again led Mrs. Treyz to the middle of the floor to reiterate a few of the basics that we had apparently seen fit to overlook. Point taken, I readied myself for another foray into defensive dancing.

This time, I was encouraged to find myself sitting almost directly across the dance floor from Martha Parks. There was something about her shyness that made her irre-sistible. Oh, what I would give to place my hand on her shoulder blade and glide around the room with her in per-fectly coordinated movements. I could just imagine what it would be like to be that close to her. I thought if I ever got the chance, I might even get up the courage to flash her a confident smile at close range. This time I would be ready to walk quickly and directly across the dance floor to her. I wouldn't let anyone push me off course or cause me to detour from my mission. This would be the dance.

Before the next dance began, however, Mr. Treyz did

something very unconventional. In a move quite uncharacteristic of his customary routine, he strode over to the boys' side of the room and asked Paul Shepard to step out of line and walk to the center of the dance floor. Leaving Paul smirking and shrugging his shoulders as the center of attention, Mr. Treyz then walked over to the row of seated girls. He held out his hand to Martha Parks, inviting her to accompany him to the middle of the floor where she joined Paul. Mr. Treyz carefully positioned Paul and Martha together, adjusting their heads and hands quite precisely, and nodded to Mrs. Treyz to place the needle on the phonograph record.

As the scratchy music began, Paul and Martha began what can only be described as gliding. Their smooth and fluid movements complemented each other perfectly as they moved as one. Mr. Treyz made a minor adjustment or two as they danced, and then stepped back to let everyone watch. *That should be me,* I thought. I'm a better dancer than Paul Shepard. I'd like to see him try that with Olive Oyl. We all watched the couple for a few minutes until Mr. Treyz politely applauded and signaled for everyone to do the same.

Then Mr. Treyz asked all of the boys to find a partner and join Paul and Martha on the dance floor. All things considered, I was a pretty good dancer. It wasn't the actual dancing that I hated so much. I just didn't like all the humiliating instruction about how to be polite and the embarrassing formalities of selecting a dance partner. With my motivation and hopes for a direct and speedy assault on Martha Parks already shattered, I slowly meandered across the floor, resigned to accept my lot in life. This time, I found myself dancing with someone named Gail. I didn't know her last name. I think she was from another school. She was kind of overweight, and I never did find her shoulder blade, but placed my right hand on a bulge that I thought came close. For a chubby girl, I thought she was quite graceful, and I did not step on her feet once.

For the next dance, Mr. and Mrs. Treyz took the floor to demonstrate the waltz. We had already learned the waltz in previous classes, but there were more advanced moves that, for some reason, they thought we were ready to attempt. While our instructors dipped and whirled, I looked up at the big clock above the basketball net at one end of the gymnasium. By my reckoning, I would have only one more chance this evening to be the first one to reach Martha Parks. Given that she had probably never noticed me, and the fact that she and Paul Shepard were now such a model couple, I could see my chances quickly dwindling. I secretly wondered if anyone had ever noticed that I always seemed to head in her direction, yet by the time I reached the far side of the room, I usually found myself standing in front of her empty chair, pretending all along to have been heading toward the girl sitting next to her. *God, I hate dancing les-sons!*

Mr. Treyz gave Mrs. Treyz one last twirl and headed toward the phonograph. This is it, I thought. I'm not letting anyone get in my way this time. This time I'll be ready. As Mr. Treyz prepared to drop the needle on the waltz track, he once again broke with convention by announcing a radical departure from our normal routine.

"This last dance will be a ladies' choice. Ladies, go find a gentleman to dance with."

"*Oh, no,*" I thought to myself. I may have even said it out loud as I hung my head forward and looked down at my penny loafers in frustration. My one last chance... Gone! A flurry of activity ensued as twenty eager girls scurried across the gymnasium toward a group of boys unaccustomed to being on the receiving end of the selection process. It felt kind of strange to just sit there while girls rushed across the room toward us and I wondered if this was how the girls felt seeing the boys jockey for position. My shyness prevented me from looking directly at them. Instead, I looked to either side, hoping my aloof attitude would hide any embarrassment were I to be the last boy chosen. Most other boys had assumed an equally nonchalant attitude, being careful not to anticipate being selected by a girl who might have her eye on the boy sitting next to him. Mary O'Neill had already asked the boy on my left to dance. And to my right, Olive Oyl, with her long stride, had been one of the first to reach my friend, Richard Lepke.

With a bustle of activity around me as boys stood to join their partners, it was becoming more difficult to pre-serve a convincing air of indifference. Now I knew what Philip Delano felt like always being the last one chosen for the softball team. Out of the corner of my eye, I became aware of a presence standing directly in front of me, and I adjusted my gaze to see a hand reaching toward... Yes, it was definitely reaching toward *me*. I took a deep breath and hoped that my face wasn't turning red. I swear, my heart almost stopped when I realized that the girl standing in front of me was Martha Parks. She smiled right at me and said something. I could see her mouth moving, but all I heard was angels singing. I don't remember saying anything back to her, but I remember standing up and following Martha out onto the dance floor thinking to myself once again how glad I was that I had remembered to wash my hands.

Without saying a word, we assumed the waltz position. When she placed her palm in mine, every molecule of my awareness rushed to my hand. It was the softest thing I had ever felt. She smelled like baby powder, and I wanted to inhale all the air around her. When the music started, we smiled at each other and slowly began to dance. Everyone else in the room disappeared, and for the next several minutes we danced and we twirled, and yes, we glided. With every turn, her honey-blonde hair brushed my right hand as it rested on her shoulder blade. Her shoulder blade, I thought, was as near to perfect as I could imagine. It was neither bony nor flabby like the two I had encountered previously. I wished that moment could have gone on forever.

I was not conscious of leading or following. It was as if each knew how the other was going to move. Once, when I thought she wasn't looking, she caught me gazing admiringly at her neck, and we both smiled. As we let the music take us in slow circles around the floor, the most surprising thought occurred to me: *God, I love dancing lessons!*

Just Going Through the Motions

I was in elementary school when President Eisenhower added the words "under God" to the Pledge of Allegiance, making an already meaningless ritual even more confounding to me. Every morning, Miss McNamara made the whole class stand beside our desks and stare at the forty-eight-star flag impaled on the wooden pole in the corner of the classroom. Then, placing our right hands over the spot where we were assured our hearts were to be found, we recited in unison the most incomprehensible, unintelligible gibberish I had ever heard.

"*I pledge allee gents.*" It seemed a curious way to begin our morning ceremony. I pictured a group of gentlemen wearing top hats, but had no idea who these "*gents*" were. And the word "*pledge*" was not yet in my vocabulary. What was I doing when I pledged these gents? Was I praying to them? Was I asking them for something like when I prayed to God and asked him for a new bike? Or was I merely greeting these gents? But I did not have time to ponder. The next few words followed too quickly to allow much time for thought.

"To the flag." I understood the words. I just didn't understand what the flag had to do with the gents I was praying to. And was I giving something *to* the flag? I knew I wasn't praying to the flag. That would be silly. I mean, it was just a flag hanging limp beside the blackboard. I had some awareness that it was identified somehow with the United States. And while it's familiar arrangement of colors hung in front of the town hall, the library, and many other buildings around town, no one ever made any reference to it other than the words we recited while holding onto our hearts.

"Of the United States of America." The words came in choppy little chunks. Each a separate, bite-size phrase entirely separate from the words before and after. That made it easy to remember, even though I was just repeating sounds. I was quite confident, however, I understood the meaning of this phrase. The United States was the country in which we all lived. This gave further credence to the fact that the flag I was staring at was somehow a symbol of this concept. It was this phrase that gave me the vague impression that I might be promising something rather than praying. But what? What was I promising to do? Did my teacher, Miss McNamara, have something to do with all of this? If I didn't keep my promise, would she tell my parents? And yet, somehow President Eisenhower was also involved. What if he found out that I had broken my promise? Was I the only one who didn't understand what was going on?

Every morning I recited a perfect, phonetically rendered version of the words I had been taught. Only occasionally did I silently question the meaning of the litany that I obediently repeated by rote along with the rest of my clueless classmates. Like everyone else, Miss McNamara was busy looking at the flag while reciting the words, so once in a while I took the opportunity to look around the room at my classmates. I hoped to discover some clue, some hint about the meaning of the perplexing ritual. Seeing only their blank stares and mechanical narration, it was quite clear that none of my friends had figured out the riddle either. No one, however, was willing to admit their ignorance and ask for clarification of the mysterious incantation.

"And to the republic." The next series of babble was already upon me. Republic was also a word that had no meaning in my young life. It was a long word—an adult word. *"Republic.. Republic."* It was rather musical, I thought. I rather enjoyed saying it, but had no conception of its meaning. I recognized the word hidden inside—*"public."* It had something to do with lots of people, mostly strangers. Like the public library or a public park. Then again, perhaps it had something to do with the even more baffling phrase that followed.

"For widget stands." This was the most perplexing of all the phrases we were forced to memorize. I had no idea what a widget was, or why it needed a stand. I could not even hazard a guess as to its obscure meaning, but for some reason, I pictured something rather small. A widget sounded like something small enough to hold in my hand. I rea-

sonably presumed that it was also somewhat important. Why else would it be on a stand? In my mind, I envisioned a kind of pedestal. Or a base like under a trophy. Or maybe they meant like a lemonade stand. No time to figure it out. Miss McNamara was saying the words with us, and I had to keep up.

"*One nation.*" I kind of rushed over those words. It was like a bridge to the next several phrases which sounded kind of like a list of some sort to me. "*One nation*" didn't really have any meaning. It just signalled that we were nearing the end of the prayer, promise, poem, magic spell, or whatever it was. I always felt myself start to speed up at these words. I was anxious to get to the end. It felt like when you're out walking your dog and he starts impatiently pulling on the leash when you start to get close to home. I couldn't wait for this thing, whatever it was, to be over so I could stop pretending I knew what I was saying and sit down. But wait! Here come the new words that the president just added to make it even longer.

"*Under God.*" These are the words that President Eisenhower wants us to say. The fact that the president had added these words made them seem really important. It also made me wonder if maybe this whole thing was a prayer after all. Why else would he add the part about God? Was I now promising something to God? Great. I'm promising something to God, and I don't even know what I'm promising. How can I keep my promise if I don't even know what I'm saying?

"*Indivisible.*" That one I know! It's like invisible, but just a more grown-up way of saying it. It means something that can't be seen. It always reminds me of ghosts or magic. I guess that's why they added the part about God. He's invisible. But everyone knows he's there. He's probably watching me right now, and he probably knows I don't understand what I'm saying.

"*With liberty.*" I don't know what this is. But now we're really getting close to the end.

"*And justice.*" I don't know what this is either. But I think it's good. It sounds like something that's important to grown-ups. It also sounds like everyone's going to get it because of what comes next.

"*For all.*" I like the way it ends. I'm not sure what it was that everyone got, but it sounds like everyone got it. "*For all.*" Yup. That sounds like everyone, alright. At least all the grown-ups, anyway. Maybe when I'm a grown-up I'll get it, too. Maybe I'll even understand what it is that everyone's getting.

My whole childhood was full of things I had to memorize and repeat. A lot of the time, I was just repeating sounds. But I made it look like I knew what it was I was saying. Sometimes there were words I understood, but they made no sense when you put them all together. The Lord's prayer was like that. "*Hollywood be thy name… Thy king done come… They will be done*" sounded very impressive and prayer-like, but, honestly, I was just faking it.

There were lots of songs that made no sense to me either. I mimicked the words, but their meanings eluded me. The one about the parts of the ram I thought I would never figure out. ("*Or the ram parts we watched were so gallantly streaming...*") And then there was the one about "*Four anber ways of grain.*"

Christmas carols had a language all their own. Even if I had known what a "*noel*" was, I had no idea what made the first one so worth singing about?

And don't even get me started on "*Round John Virgin.*"

"Oh, You Shouldn't Have"

She was a retired third-grade school teacher. She was also a spinster. But the word that might have best described Aunt Lois was "eccentric." Whether by choice or accidental circumstance, she lived alone all the way out in Indiana in a house none of us ever got to see. I met her only a few times in my life. Once when she came east to join us on vacation up in Maine, and once... well, I actually don't remember meeting her on any other occasion. I only assume because she was my grandfather's sister, that perhaps I had seen her once or twice before I was old enough to remember anyone who was not feeding me or changing my diapers.

What I remember about the one time I do recall meeting her is that she looked remarkably like my grandfather in drag. Already well on her way to becoming elderly, her shock of ink-black hair, while not making her look any younger, did succeed in making her look like an old lady trying to look younger. It was probably not her real hair, as thick, black waves covered the hairline on all sides, concealing any evidence that the material might not actually have originated from her scalp. It was a stiff and lifeless matte that had the synthetic sheen of something manufactured rather than grown. You got the feeling that in a stiff breeze the entire assembly might have fluttered tentatively, attempting to lift off like an overloaded cargo plane on a long runway.

On one particularly hot day during our trip to Maine, she hiked two miles to the tackiest part of Old Orchard Beach. She found herself on a sleazy, commercial strip typical of those found in similar beach resort towns, and before any of us knew she was gone, she had returned carrying thirteen pounds of fudge. Wedged between a T-shirt shop and a pinball arcade, she had discovered one of those touristy establishments that specializes in selling an infinite variety of a single item. Their narrow focus, but extensive selection of inventory is usually implied right in their name: Sunglass World, House of Sandals, Bikini Heaven, Sea Shell Paradise, Cheese-A-Rama.

World-O-Fudge apparently proved too tempting for Aunt Lois to resist. There, displayed in glass cases right along the sidewalk were sheets of fudge of every conceivable description luring tourists into a sugary stupor. In full view of pedestrians, giant copper vats of molten chocolate were stirred with wooden spoons by men wearing white paper hats and clean, pressed aprons. By the time Aunt Lois left World-O-Fudge, she was the proud owner of thirteen different varieties. A virtual smorgasbord of fudge.

That night after dinner, she unveiled her hoard with great ceremony, but only after first establishing a systematic set of rules and regulations for its consumption. I had hoped, though unrealistically, we might each be allowed simply to take a piece and politely nibble on it while displaying our best manners and infinite gratitude—something Aunt Lois seemed to thrive on. She had a way of minimizing her own efforts on our behalf, while at the same time encouraging our continued indebtedness.

"Mmmm, delicious fudge! Thank you, Aunt Lois. That was very thoughtful of you."

"Oh, you're welcome. I was happy to walk two miles in the stifling heat to bring you a morsel of candy. And I'm sure the blisters on my feet will heal in no time."

But that was too much to ask. It became a kind of class project that seemed to drag on for an eternity. I guess once a third-grade teacher, always a third-grade teacher. And Aunt Lois had center stage. She unwrapped each package, carefully placing it in the middle of the dining table, and with great fanfare, introduced each flavor as if she were announcing debutantes at a fancy ball.

"Chocolate Mint... Maple Walnut... Penuche... Peanut Butter Delight..." Following each pronouncement she would pause for the expected chorus of ooohs and mmmms. "Vanilla Swirl..." ("ooooh"), "Coconut Mocha..." ("mmmm"). The tedious process went on and on. There was brown fudge, beige fudge, green fudge. One, I swear, was the exact color of Pepto-Bismol, but I didn't catch the name of that particular flavor. I was busy trying to think of variations on our exclamations of anticipated pleasure that were by now growing predictably repetitious. "Wow... Hooray... Eureka!"

At long last, the final box of fudge—Double Dutch Chocolate Marshmallow—was revealed, and we had spread before us within arm's reach our own private World-O-Fudge. But we were not yet allowed to touch. Fudge class with Aunt Lois was just getting started. Before the exercise would be deemed complete, each family member at the table would be asked to sample a carefully rationed portion of each variety, and then be required to explain to the rest of the group which one was our favorite and why. With ten of us seated at the table, I did a quick calculation of the time it would take for this little drill to run its course, and wondered if it was too late to ask for a second helping of meat-loaf to tide me over.

By the time my sister, Katharine, had completed her dissertation extolling the superior attributes of Creme de Menthe, I was half expecting the next portion of the assignment to require written essays on each variety, at which point I had planned to fake a bout of nausea and excuse myself from the gathering. I would have to be the first to make such a declaration, however. Being the second person to feign such an attack would certainly arouse suspicion. And, if it came to that, I wondered if I would be required to raise my hand and wait to be called upon before asking for permission to be excused.

The following day, the tedium of fudge analysis thank-fully behind us, Aunt Lois temporarily diverted attention away from her startlingly youthful hair by appearing on the beach wearing shorts. Forced to guess, I'd say that her legs had not seen the sun since, perhaps, the Truman administration. If it were possible to make her hair look any blacker, two of the whitest legs I have ever seen did the trick. A lavish display of spidery, blue veins added to the effect, and made it seem as if she were balancing on two rolled-up roadmaps.

"Don't you think you should put some sunblock on your legs?" my mother noted with some alarm.

I shared her concern and, while I thought long pants or a heavy blanket would have been more appropriate, I kept quiet and secretly wondered if my grandfather's legs bore any similarity.

But her uncanny portrayal of my grandfather as a woman and her wearisome ability to turn dessert into a homework assignment was not what made Aunt Lois so uniquely memorable. Aunt Lois really came into her own during the Christmas holiday season. She will be forever remembered for making Christmas the hilarious celebration of poor taste that my family looked forward to each year. About a week before each Christmas, a notice in our mailbox would alert us to the fact that we had received a package from Indiana that was too large for our mailbox, and that we could pick it up at the post office at our convenience.

The anticipation of Aunt Lois's Christmas package was almost too much to bear. It was something that for weeks leading up to the holiday, we looked forward to with a strange combination of excitement and dread. Now that it had arrived, even Mom and Dad became almost giddy at the prospect of opening the presents, and all other household activity was put on hold for the ritual. Hers were the only presents we were allowed to open before Christmas, knowing that they would undoubtedly be the most memorable. For her gifts to attain this high level of distinction was truly an extraordinary feat on Aunt Lois's part considering the fact that during the many years in which she sent us packages, she never once bought us a single present. She succeeded in bypassing this needless step by giftwrapping whatever she had lying around the house and felt she had no use for. In this regard, Aunt Lois was ahead of her time, having anticipated the trend toward recycling and re-gifting that would not become popular for decades to come.

In a disturbing way, Aunt Lois's Christmas presents made you feel special and privileged because you knew that no one else on the entire planet was getting the exact same gift. Your gift was unique in all the world. A one-of-a-kind sentiment chosen specifically for you. But it wasn't as if she searched her house for perfectly good items that she simply could not use—a scarf that was not her style, a second travel alarm clock. This practice, though odd, would have been entirely understandable. She apparently, however, giftwrapped items just seconds before they were to be thrown into the trash, in some cases, perhaps just seconds after being retrieved *from* the trash. It was as if she kept a roll of Christmas wrapping paper right beside her rubbish bin for those frequent occasions when she stopped short and said to herself, "On second thought, that nearly used-up bar of soap would be just the thing for my nephew, David."

Actually, it was my sister, Lulu, who had the honor of receiving the used bar of soap. That was the same year I received a collection of pencil nubs that had been worn down to the size of cigarette butts. All but a few bore the teeth marks of former owners, and their erasers had been worn flat, attending to the misspellings of eight-year-olds. My sister, Katharine, got a half-depleted box of Kotex pads, while Mom, that year, unwrapped the grand prize. That was the year Mom received a douche bag. Not just any douche bag, a *used* douche bag.

If the measure of the perfect gift is one that is never forgotten, then Aunt Lois was the supreme gifter. Although I never visited her home, I had formed a mental picture over the years of what must surely be a monument to bad taste and an accumulation of items once destined for the trash which never quite arrived, but were detoured instead to holding bins marked "Family Christmas Gifts." I pictured a split-level house in the middle of a nondescript block of similar homes, identical except for one of those ceramic kittens climbing on her roof. The artificial Christmas tree in her front picture window and the giant, colored glass ball atop a pedestal on her lawn would make everything all seem quite normal. It always seemed more intriguing to me that one might drive down her street never suspecting that behind her monogrammed, aluminum storm door existed a bizarre world where an eccentric old lady, instead of throwing things away, giftwrapped and mailed them to loved ones.

Opening a present that had once been in her house felt like snooping through someone's closets and bureau drawers when they weren't home. Crammed into a cedar chest I imagined finding hundreds of items that students had at one time given her as end-of-school-year gifts. Unopened bottles of dime store cologne, cheap knick-knacks marked "made in Japan," countless tins of talcum powder, and stacks of hankies. In the back of a closet I'd come across boxes of items confiscated from unruly students, and anything that had been left behind in their desks at the end of the year. I'm sure if I dug deep enough I'd find ancient spitballs, wadded-up chewing gum, and half-eaten Tootsie Rolls. I thought, perhaps, I might even discover huge, petrified blocks of fudge left over from previous mid-term assignments.

Mom always made us write "thank-you" notes to Aunt Lois. Not only because it was the polite thing to do, but also because it would help encourage the receipt of an equally tasteless shipment the following year. Mom usually read our notes before sending them to make sure we hadn't written anything as inappropriate as Aunt Lois's presents. Thank-you notes were sometimes a challenge to write and they helped me, I'm sure, to develop my creative writing skills. You tend to run out of glowing adjectives about chewed-up pencil stubs after you've already used the words "delightful" and "extraordinary." Had she been there in person (something I was always grateful was not the case) I wondered if she would have perceived the clever double meaning in the phrase that I always imagined myself saying to her: "Oh, Aunt Lois. You shouldn't have."

Before she died, Aunt Lois wrote to my parents to ask them if it would be okay if she left them money in her will. There was little chance that my parents would have declined her generosity had she not had the foresight to ask. It would be the only thing she ever gave them that wasn't half-used or ready to be thrown away. But by asking in advance, she was able to collect the attendant thank-yous without the unfortunate side effect of actually having to die. Having no close relatives or children, her church would become the recipient of her entire house and its contents, along with the tedious responsibility of having to go through her entire house and its contents. All things considered, my parents got the better end of the deal.

When Aunt Lois died, her passing was merely a footnote to an otherwise uneventful Tuesday. I remembered meeting her just once, and the fact that I would never see her again had little impact except for the fact that it marked the end of a long tradition. It meant the end of truly tasteless Christmas presents. There would be no more hilarious laughter at the prospect of giftwrapped trash. No more stunned silence upon unwrapping a partially used box of personal hygiene products or out-of-style, used shoes.

Call me sentimental, but I will never again be able to look at a used douche bag without thinking of Aunt Lois.

Are We There Yet?

Cars were different when I was a kid. I don't mean different from what they are now. That goes without saying. The cars of that post-war era were extravagant displays of excess and flamboyant celebrations of chrome. After years of sacrifice in the war effort, their massive bulk and excessive decoration were testament to a renewed prosperity and decadence. You don't have to look far to see that things have changed over the years. But that's not what I'm talking about.

No, when I say cars were different, I mean different from each other. As in "unique." As in "not clones." When I was a kid, there was no mistaking a Ford for a Chevy, or a Buick for a Pontiac. Not only did each have its own separate character and style, but every year the cars were completely redesigned. There was no mistaking a '57 Chevy, for example, for a '58 Chevy. They were two entirely different cars. No two visible parts were the same from year to year. It was Detroit's way of making sure that Americans never became too complacent driving last year's models. I could just hear our neighbors, Mr. and Mrs. Dean, gushing about the impressive features of their brand new Galaxie 500. "Oh, and Frank and I just fell in love with the stylish vinyl roof. It's all the latest rage, you know. It looks like a convertible, but without the inconvenience of actually having to be out in that dreadful wind."

The new models actually came out in September. It was as if they couldn't bear to go full-term and were born prematurely into an expectant world. My friends and I took great delight in seeing them unveiled across glossy, double-page spreads in *Life* magazine, and imagined which of the new models we would purchase if we had the disposable income and had we not been nine years old. For months afterward, seeing a new car parked on the street was a noteworthy event. We all got off our bikes and walked around the new model pointing out the new chrome embellishments or the redesigned shape of the grille and taillights. No detail was so small that it escaped our detection. New meant *new*. Not the same as last year's with a slightly altered trunk medallion.

The few exceptions to this rule brought disappointment to my small circle of friends who waited all year to see what innovations and new automobile fashion trends the new model year would bring. The 1954 Chevrolet, for example, looks almost exactly the same as the 1953 Chevrolet. It made me wonder what the car designers at Chevy had been doing since issuing the previous year's models. Had they worked for a whole year at their drawing boards and come up empty? What had they been doing during the entire time it took me to get through the second grade? And who was it exactly that determined that those new designs were so bad that the company would be better off repeating last year's models but with slightly different hubcaps? If the 1959 Chevrolet is to be used as a benchmark, the designs we *didn't* get to see must have been atrocious.

When I was a kid, my parents always bought used cars. Cars that had once been new, but had spent their youth with another family, transporting them to the beach or on vacation to far-off and interesting destinations. I tried to imagine the exciting places they had gone together that we would never know about. By the time we got the cars, they were in their adolescent years. Certainly not old age, or even adulthood for that matter. But they had lost that new-car smell years before being cast aside like orphans for fancier and more youthful models. I had heard people refer to that new-car smell, but having never experienced it as a child, it was left entirely to my imagination. Pressing my nose to the seat covers of our new, used car, I tried to imagine the same smell, only more intense. If this is what everyone was raving about, I thought, I don't see what all the fuss is about. By the time we got to take our first ride in any of our cars, they usually smelled like Lysol with subtle undertones of dog. The maiden voyage was always exciting, nevertheless, and my sister and I insisted that Dad drive past all of our friends' houses honking the horn as we waved through the beautiful tinted windows. I usually spent the next week sitting in the front seat in our driveway fantasizing that I was old enough to drive, or pointing out the five-year-old, but still relatively innovative, features to my buddies.

"And there's this little tab under the rearview mirror that you can flip if the headlights behind you are too bright," I bragged.

"All cars have that now," my unimpressed friend, Kenny, noted.

"And then if you pull this, it sprays water onto the windshield to clean it," I added, pretending not to hear his comments, and leaving a drizzle of sudsy liquid to run down onto the hood.

So acutely atuned were my friends and I to style changes in the auto industry, that we tried to get our parents to update their cars' accessories whenever possible. The year that parking lights changed from white lenses to amber, a couple of cheap yellow bulbs was all it took to bring our old car right up to date with current trends. When our '61 Chevrolet Parkwood needed new tires, I pleaded my case to have them replaced with the stylish, thinner whitewalls that were now in vogue, rather than the wide and dated originals. My friend, Dennis, had the same idea, but his parents were reluctant to spend the extra money on any form of frivolous decoration. For him, the thought of being seen in a used Rambler was bad enough, but a Rambler with blackwall tires was too much for Dennis to bear. He finally succeeded in talking them into buying a set of fake whitewalls.

For considerably less than the cost of the real thing, one could purchase a set of flat, rubber sidewalls with a wide, white border at their outer edge. They fit over the existing tires like flat life preservers, and were held in place by the wheel rims. Stretch them over the rims, snap the hubcaps back on, and voila! You're right in style! Kind of like spats. Or a clip-on necktie. They were pretty convincing except at speeds over fifty miles per hour, when they had a tendency to lift and flutter, causing the people in the cars you were passing to point at them while mouthing words to you. "Your... tires ... are ... flaaaapping!"

After a year or so, the fake whitewalls on the old Rambler started to warp and buckle, causing them to resemble a record album that someone had left out in the hot sun. The only thing worse than people seeing that you had blackwall tires was people seeing that you had blackwall tires that you tried to disguise. The day Dennis's father asked him to get rid of the imitation whitewalls, we had planned to go to the movies in the next town. I helped him expose the bland tire underbellies by removing what had become known to all the neighborhood kids as tire toupees. Then he asked me if I thought my mom would mind driving us to the theatre in her car.

Throughout my childhood years, cars grew larger and larger. Their dinosaur-like torsos sheathed in heavy armor plating became a sign of success and prosperity. Americans embraced their oversized behemoths as an appropriate expression of excess in which to cruise the new superhighways that were beginning to stretch across the country. Wheel bases became longer and wider, and dashboard instrumentation began to resemble a hybrid of an airplane cockpit and a jukebox. In 1958, double sets of headlights became the norm, and older cars with only a single headlight on each side became dated and kind of forlorn-looking. Chrome appendages became sculptural statements of immoderation, and the sheer enormity of automobiles attained epic proportions. I peered into the vast cavity under the open hood of a friend's family Oldsmobile, and thought it only slightly smaller than my parents' double bed. The trunk compartment dwarfed the spare tire and could have conceivably accommodated my entire little league team. More, bigger, and better was clearly the new rule.

My mother's uncle, Erwin, was the first in our family to buy a brand-new car. It was a Cadillac. White with giant fins projecting off the back fenders and out into space. The fins had no practical purpose other than to hold aloft an impressive array of taillights. The first day he showed it off to the family, he drove small groups of us around the block, as we pretended to be wealthy speculators who had come to buy up all the neighborhood property and turn it into a high-rent office park.

Small battalions of relatives took turns clamoring into the spacious interior. It was like an enormous room with two giant sofas. From the back seat, the people sitting up front seemed hopelessly distant for any meaningful interaction without having to raise your voice. So this is what that new-car smell is all about, I thought to myself. It was kind of like... sticking your head into a package of Wonder Bread, and then into a fresh tin of Band-Aids. Not entirely unpleasant, but nothing I'd go out of my way to seek out.

I played with the controls for the power windows in the back hoping that strangers we passed on the street would notice me. "Look at that lucky boy," I imagined them saying. "I'd give anything to be so privileged—to live in such luxury. He must be filthy rich." For three minutes that day, I was.

It was the only time I ever got to ride in Erwin's Cadillac. There were times, however, when he visited that I stood beside it in our driveway or leaned against one of its huge fenders with a familiarity that suggested a privileged upbringing. I imagined passersby staring in envy at my mere proximity to such obvious wealth, hoping that they might one day ascend to my level of social status. Looking back, it is more probable that they were wondering if the car's owner knew that some grubby little kid was getting fingerprints all over his new car.

The following year, tail fins grew even larger, chassis swelled to even grander proportions, and Erwin's big Cadillac suddenly became last year's model. It was all part of Detroit's plan. The molds and machinery that had been used to form the distinct shape of Erwin's magnificent automobile were retired and abandoned, except perhaps, for the manufacture of replacement parts for what were now the older models. Everything about the new Caddies was completely different. The body shape had been totally redefined. The new grille shattered the previous limits of overdesign. More chrome was added in more places. The dashboard, the side mirrors, the bumpers, the hood ornament, even the wheel covers of a year ago were completely trashed in favor of the luxurious, "all-new" Cadillac. It was as if its designers were saying, "No, wait. We have an even better idea. That stuff we told you last year about being the ultimate expression of elegance and style? Forget that."

Of course, you had to take what the car ads were saying with a grain of salt. Every year the magazine ad headlines tried to outdo the year before. It was like a game of "I can top that," and I wondered when they would finally run out of superlative expressions.

Even as a child it was easy to see how car ads were exaggerated. The pictures, for example, were all lies. In order to make the cars look larger than they actually were, they populated them with miniature, pinhead families whose tiny craniums would have been no larger than a potato were they to be suddenly brought to life. The miniature people in the cars were always dressed in their Sunday best and smiling broadly at one another, just happy to be alive and in each others' company. Pinhead Dad, sitting behind an enormous steering wheel, wears a tiny fedora hat to match his tiny suit and tie. Beside him, a devoted Pinhead Mom beams at the prospect that her husband is able to afford such

a beautiful, new car. Or maybe she's just happy to be out of the house. It was hard to tell exactly from the picture. Either way, the ad was not a portrayal of real life.

Meanwhile, Buddy and Sis Pinhead sit in back, their miniature bodies nearly lost in the vastness of the enormous rear compartment. The ad depicts enough room for a dance floor between the back seat and Mom and Dad up front. All lies. I know this for a fact to be an extreme exaggeration because whenever I acted up in the back seat (which I almost never did), my dad could easily reach around the back of his seat and give me a good swat with the back of his hand. All without taking his eyes off the road. The well-behaved children in the ad, of course, never needed discipline. Sis, in a crisp, party dress, buries her tiny head quietly in a book probably years beyond the average reading level of other kids her age. Buddy smiles gleefully out the back window at something the car is evidently passing. The ad doesn't show you what exactly. That is left up to your imagination. By his delighted expression, I pictured maybe a tiny dog humping another on the sidewalk, or peeing on a nice bed of flowers. These were two well-behaved children who, even after hours in the spacious back seat, had never whined the words, "Are we there yet?"

At any rate, everything in car ads was exaggerated. Not only to make the cars appear much bigger than they actually were, but also to give one the impression that the privilege of riding around in a nice, new car, like the one in the ad, could turn your family into a reasonably functional unit that could sit in close proximity for an hour or more without becoming physically violent.

My sister and I were pretty well-behaved as kids go. We made up a lot of games and played them quietly on long trips until one accused the other of cheating. Sometimes Mom and Dad would join us and we'd all play the game together. A game we particularly enjoyed was going through the alphabet in order and spotting things that began with "a, b, c, d ..." and so on. Having anticipated this activity before a particularly lengthy trip, I once came up with a strategy designed to ensure my overwhelming victory. When Mom suggested that we play the alphabet game, I eagerly accepted, telling her what a good idea I thought it was, and further explaining that I had forgotten all about that game. Before anyone else had the chance to even begin to look for an airplane, an ambulance, or an aardvark, I began reciting my rehearsed, alphabetical litany, pointing to various parts of myself. "Arm, belly, chin, dimple... (here I had to pause long enough to smile and display one of my most endearing features), elbow, finger, gap... (another pause to point out my missing front tooth), hand..."

I had gotten only up to about "knee" when my sister, Kathy, interrupted. "Mom, he's cheating!"

"No, I'm not! Everything is right here. Elbow... hand. See?" As I held my various parts in her face for closer inspection, the exchange quickly escalated into a shouting match.

The game was temporarily suspended while the rules committee in the front seat amended the official regulations. "No body parts. And nothing inside the car." Just as well, I thought. I had not been able to come up with anything for "q" and "x," and had not been entirely sure that "vertebra" would be accepted, since you couldn't actually see it.

As the game resumed, I sat smugly, having undeniably demonstrated my intellectual superiority. We continued on our journey as we all peered out the car windows searching for something beginning with the next letter. A normal-sized family with normal-sized heads, wearing normal-sized clothing. And in back of our parents, my sister and I, on our best behavior, sat on a normal-sized back seat within easy reach of Dad's quick swat.

A Very Silent Night

Lust, greed, pain, temptation, torture. God, I love Christmas! The year was 1953. Christmas Eve. I stood at the top of our front stairway looking down along the banister toward the front door. A streetlight cast a pale glow onto the wide floorboards in the front hall of 294 Central Street. It was 3:00 a.m.

Christmas had already arrived in the rooms downstairs. I could sense it. My parents had forbidden my sister and me to encroach on what surely lay waiting for us under the decorated tree. We were to wait until the whole family had awakened and had gathered at the upstairs landing. Then, and only then, would our slippered feet pad down the staircase in unison. Mom and Dad had instructed us not to awaken them, as, presumably, my two-month-old baby sister's nighttime feeding would allow them only intermittent sleep. Tempted as I was to do otherwise, I would wait patiently at the top landing while the rest of the house slept in hushed darkness.

Time dragged painfully slowly. How anyone could sleep through the anticipation was beyond me. I had tried. Lying

69

quietly under my Roy Rogers bedspread and closing my eyes, the excitement made it impossible to drift off to sleep. My mind would drift instead slowly down the stairs and into the living room. I tried to imagine what colorful bounty awaited me. My eyes opened repeatedly, hoping to catch the first dim light of a dawn that seemed hopelessly far off. My mind was racing, and sleep seemed like something I could not remember how to achieve. It was torture.

And so I waited. Standing quietly on the landing, I looked down across the banister railing where we had hung our Christmas stockings. Since we had no fireplace, and thus, no mantel, the banister was the place we could access most quickly on our way downstairs when critical seconds mattered. Ever since I can remember, we had hung my mother's stockings on Christmas Eve. Not the Christmas-colored stockings that grandmothers knit, but the shriveled brown nylons worn by most women of the 1950s. The kind that snagged on your fingers as you pushed your hand in reaching for Santa's gifts. They weren't pretty, but a single orange placed in the toe of such a stocking stretched it out to about as tall as I was. And that meant a lot of stocking to fill with goodies. Of course, Santa quickly figured out that a rolled-up ten-cent comic book filled almost a foot of it.

From my dark perch atop the front stairway, I could barely make out shadowy forms protruding over the handrail where just hours before, the stockings hung limp and empty. I could see they now had been filled to overflowing, straining under the weight of wonderful surprises. Not for hours, however, would there be enough light to identify any of the intriguing shapes.

Our house was one of the oldest in our small New England town, and the wooden structure creaked and groaned under the weight of snow. Sounds that on any normal night might have seemed frightening, were not the least bit scary tonight. Even in the darkness, the entire house remained friendly and welcoming, and silhouettes of Christmas decorations were all around. The colorless shapes of little plastic reindeer and a sleigh stood quietly aligned on the windowsill where I waited. I knew that with the arrival of daylight, the sleigh would once again take on its familiar bright red coloring, and the chipped red paint on Rudolph's nose would again be evident. The whole miniature scene on its bed of white cotton snow provided a constant reminder of the reason for my lonely vigil.

The broad sill came up to my young chest, and I leaned my elbows on it for support. Looking through the frosty, double window past the tiny plastic figures, I could see the row of streetlights get smaller as it stretched toward the nearby town center. I watched as a snow plow scraped by, the sound of its wide metal blade curiously muffled by snow that continued to fall. Snowflakes spiraled in the yellow glow cast off from its headlights. How strange it was to see someone who was not at home asleep like the rest of our quiet neighborhood. It was the middle of the night on Christmas Eve, and someone was outside as if it were no night in particular. Had he been driving around all night?

Had he seen Santa? The reindeer would be easy to spot in this snow, especially with no one else about. Surely the driver must have seen something.

I watched as the snow plow came to a silent stop at the end of our street and paused for nonexistent cars. The driver made a left turn, and I watched until he was out of sight. Sitting down on the top step, I once again looked down toward the stockings. Time seemed to almost stand still. Should I crawl into bed again? I could not imagine calming my excitement enough to fall asleep, and I was surprised to find I was not the least bit sleepy for having stayed awake so long past bedtime.

All things considered, I suppose I was a pretty obedient child. There were nights, however, when bedtime arrived as an unwelcome deadline. I'm sure I put up a fuss once in a while when the curfew seemed not only early, but arbitrary. Why was I not allowed to cross over that mysterious line delineating awake time from sleep time? My entire life thus far had been spent in awake time, and I knew what to expect. But what happened on the other side of that magic hour was still very much a mystery. What shape the world took after awake time had drawn to a close I could only imagine. It was a world where grown-ups lived and little children were too tired to follow. The more adamant my parents were about my bedtime, the more significant it became. So it came as somewhat of a surprise this night to find that the hours after my bedtime were not markedly different from those that came before it. Aside from the dark quiet, things were pretty much the same. Certainly nothing of significance was happening here.

Wait. A sound. It was coming from my parents room. Yes, something was definitely stirring. I held my breath in order to hear the faint sounds. Did they feel sorry for me sitting all alone on the landing and decide that I shouldn't be made to wait any longer? Could we all go downstairs now and begin to unwrap our presents? I listened with more intensity than I knew I had. There it was again, but louder. It was my baby sister, Lorene. I could tell by her wimpers that she was not fully awake. Maybe her sounds would get louder and Mom and Dad would wake up. Then they'd figure since they were awake anyway we might as well all go downstairs and finally begin Christmas. It would be no use trying to get back to sleep on such a momentous morning.

Unable to hold my breath any longer, I exhaled and slowly drew another. The sounds had stopped. Again the house fell into a long silence. The harder I listened the more quiet it seemed to get. Several minutes passed. Then came a sound once again. This time from outside. It was another snow plow. This time, I didn't bother to stand up to look out the window. I sat listening until the coarse metallic sound grew faint. Then it was gone.

The abrupt jerk of my head falling forward indicated to me that I had dozed off. My shoulder pressed against the printed wallpaper where I had propped myself up. How

long had I been asleep? I traced the cracks of the floorboards on the top step with my finger. How many times had
I crossed them on my way up or down. Yet I had never really noticed them. Never had I studied them close up as I did
now. The square, handmade nails were worn smooth from
two centuries of comings and goings. What other families
had called this home? What other children had sat on this
very spot waiting for Santa?

Santa! Right. For a moment I actually forgot why I
found myself slumped in this unlikely corner of the stairway.
What awaited me downstairs under the tree? The Sears catalog this year had been exceptionally large, and packed with
so much that I had wanted. I could imagine coasting down
the snow-covered hill out back on a brand-new flying
saucer. Every kid in the neighborhood would want to be me.

Had Santa brought me what I had asked for? And without a fireplace, how did he get into our house? The front
door seemed a likely possibility, but I couldn't conjure up
the scene in my mind—Santa opening our storm door and
squeezing through past the hall radiator with his big sack. It
was no picture I'd ever seen on a Christmas card, or in a picture book. But the answers to these questions didn't matter
tonight. There were presents downstairs waiting to be
unwrapped. How they got into our living room was of little
concern.

Besides, it was beginning to look a little lighter.
Shadowy profiles of items downstairs were beginning to
identify themselves. There's my father's coat hanging just

inside the door. And those are my snow boots in the corner. Was that something green sticking up through the reinforced band at the top of my mother's nylon stocking? I could see a little more detail through the window at the bottom of the stairs, too. The light snow cover made everything a little brighter, and familiar landmarks took on rounded, pale white forms. I could now tell it was definitely approaching the hour at which the rest of my family would awaken and we'd all rumble down the stairs in our pajamas.

As I squinted, trying to make out which stocking was mine, I became aware of movement coming from slightly behind where I sat. Turning, but not startled, I quickly identified the small bare feet standing next to me as those of my five-year-old sister, Kathy. She was chattering excitedly about toys, and was already three steps past me before I caught her hand, reminding her of our promise to wait. I shushed her, but her enthusiasm grew louder at the sight of bulging stockings. I gently pulled her back up to the top step, and wordlessly motioned for her to sit. But even before she had been persuaded to do so, my parents' bedroom door opened and Mom and Dad emerged. After gathering in a hushed excitement on the landing, we all trundled downstairs, grabbing our stockings on the way, and entering the living room to a general chorus of oohs and aahs.

And so it began. Christmas 1953. I can't say that I remember the day. Or what presents I waited so long to unwrap. That Christmas day has faded into the past, blending together with so many others. But many decades later, the hours leading up to that one Christmas, the hours I spent on the top step on that very silent night is one of my most vivid memories of childhood. And so it remains to this day, that for me, the anticipation of Christmas always outshines the day itself. The excitement of looking forward, and the nostalgia of looking back always seems larger than life. Like the hours after my childhood bedtime, the day itself is not that different from others. Once it arrives, you realize it's filled with the same mundane events that mark every other day. You shower, you get dressed. There are meals to be cooked, dishes to wash, and trash to remove.

Yes, for me, the best part of Christmas isn't Christmas. It's waiting for it to arrive. My nights of waiting for Santa may be past. Being with family and friends is now most important. The excitement is in the planning and preparation. The joy of giving has surpassed the joy of receiving. But every December, from somewhere deep inside of me, I am reminded of a little boy sitting on the top step. Waiting. He is every child. And at Christmas we are again, all of us, children.

No Place Like the Drive-in

Nearly every summer night shortly before midnight, I was awakened by a parade that formed along the length of the quiet street in front of our house. I was seven years old with a bedtime of, perhaps, eight o'clock, and often came to the upstairs window to watch a steady stream of bumper-to-bumper automobiles stretching as far as I could see crawl past the house. After the last of the ten-minute procession of cars had finally filtered through the intersection in the center of town, the street once again fell silent and I crawled back into bed. This nightly ritual went on all summer long, weather permitting.

The parade originated about two miles to the north of our house and dissipated as it reached the intersection just beyond, where the cars turned in various directions to make their way home along the dark streets of our small New England town. This late-night phenomenon coincided with the conclusion of the movie at the Nashoba Drive-in Theater, as hundreds of automobiles spilled simultaneously out onto Central Street. I watched the long, slow procession of cars pass and enviously wondered what movie people had been watching while I was sound asleep. During the 1950s, parades like this were taking place all over small-town America, as more families began to enjoy automobile-related pastimes, and the number of drive-ins soared to over four thousand.

Occasionally, we were lucky enough to actually take part in the late-night parade when my sister and I begged repeatedly, "Pleeeeease, can we go to the drive-in tonight?" and pestered my parents long enough to wear down any initial resistance there might have been.

"Ask your father," Mom would eventually reply. When Dad finally responded with a grin and a "we'll see," we knew we were on our way. At our house, "we'll see" always meant "yes," and was our cue to stop badgering and begin displaying our best behavior. The concession was often accompanied by a caveat like, "only if you eat all of your vegetables." Choking down four mouthfuls of string beans seemed an acceptable price to pay for a night at the drive-in.

The drive-in was only a couple of miles or so up the street, but to us, it was a big outing. When we piled into our 1941 Plymouth, my sister and I were already in our pajamas, as it would already be past our bedtimes by the time it was dark enough for the movie to begin. Three minutes after leaving our driveway, we were pulling up to the kiosk at the drive-in entrance where an attendant leaned out of the small booth with his hand extended. Admission was a dollar a car. It didn't matter to my sister and me what movie was playing. The novelty of viewing it on a giant outdoor screen was adventure enough regardless of what it was we were viewing.

Driving up and down the rows of cars, Dad searched for the best place to stake our claim. There was an art to selecting the perfect space, and Dad considered himself an expert at weighing all the criteria for selection. He insisted on being as close to the middle of the screen as possible so that the projected image would not be distorted. But not too close to the front where we'd be looking up at too extreme an angle. And if we parked too close to the restrooms or snackbar, we'd have a steady stream of people passing beside our car for the duration of the show.

Dad also took into consideration the cars parked beside us. Better to slip into a space between two already positioned cars with nice-looking families or even an elderly couple if you could locate one. Pulling into a slot with empty spaces on either side, you could wind up beside a carload of noisy teenagers or a crying baby. It was always preferable to choose your neighbors rather than to let them choose you. You couldn't leave anything to chance when it came to something this important. Other people were also looking for spaces, so it felt a little like musical chairs, but we were confident in Dad's ability to position us where we would receive the most strategic advantages. Some drivers considered it more important to be toward the back or the side to facilitate an easy exit when the movie ended, but it was a trade-off, and Dad always had our best interests at heart.

This time we lucked out. We pulled in just between two elderly ladies in an old Buick and a nice-looking young couple in a station wagon. We slipped head-first into the coveted space just as another dad was eyeing it from the other side and appeared ready to cut us off.

Raised mounds of gravel running the length of each row like a giant washboard allowed cars to tilt upward at an appropriate angle for optimal viewing. Metal posts every two spaces held bulky speakers that lifted off their stands and attached to the front side window by means of a metal bracket. The speakers looked like small outboard motors and sounded like someone speaking through a garden hose. But it didn't matter. We were at the drive-in and the adventure of it made up for any shortcomings in comfort and viewing quality.

We had barely settled into our parking space when my sister and I were already weaving our way between the rows of cars toward the front of the open field where a small playground awaited. The modest assortment of swings and see-saws was dwarfed by the huge, white monolith looming up behind them. Seeing the screen from this close with all of its flaws and imperfections always seemed very peculiar to me, and it was difficult to imagine that it would soon be magically transformed into a whole other dimension, causing its creases and dents to disappear.

By quarter of nine, carloads of patrons anxious for the movie to start showed their impatience by turning on their headlights, illuminating the bottom half of the blank screen as a discordant chorus of honking horns underscored their demand. The headlights projected silhouettes of the playground onto the bottom of the screen like shadow puppets, and I always enjoyed identifying my own silhouette by waving or making other spastic movements. It was like being in a two-dimensional movie, and I wondered if people in their cars noticed how perilously high I was able to swing while still managing to wave frantically.

As enthralling as this was, impending darkness was our cue to begin searching for the family car—always a challenge in the fading light of evening. We were usually several rows off in our calculation of where our parents had last been seen, and always seemed to end up wandering aimlessly up and down between each row of cars along with a dozen or so other dazed-looking children who had been temporarily orphaned by the daunting landscape of vehicles. Occasionally, we passed the same kids we had just seen several minutes before, but walking in the opposite direction. After a while, a set of headlights would flash and my dad's voice would call, "Kids, stop fooling around and get in the car." We never actually confessed to being lost, but explained that we just felt like getting a little exercise before we had to climb into the back seat.

My sister and I always welcomed the previews of coming attractions that preceded the feature because it gave us a chance to plead our case for another outing to the drive-in.

"Pleeeease ... can we see that movie too?" We waited for

a "we'll see," but usually had to settle for a "shhhh."

Tonight's movie was *The Long, Long Trailer* starring Lucille Ball and Desi Arnaz. They played newlyweds who, rather than buying a house, decided to travel around the country pulling an enormous mobile home. It was pretty funny, especially when Lucille Ball tried to cook dinner in a moving trailer. She spilled food all over the place as she was thrown from one side of the trailer to the other. We couldn't stop laughing.

Viewing a drive-in movie from the back seat had its disadvantages. From a sitting position, the bottom of the screen was cut off, so for the most part, my sister and I stood in back of our parents, chins resting on our arms which were folded in front of us on the wide bench seat. Mohair upholstery could be pretty itchy on your skin, so rather than hear us complain, Mom often thought to bring towels to drape over the back of the front seat. We took turns standing in the middle on the hump over the drive shaft where neither parent's head obstructed our view. However, because all cars built in the 1940s had divided windshields, standing in the middle also had its drawbacks, and we frequently alternated positions, causing a minor commotion in the back seat as we traded complaints of unfairness. "Mom, he's hogging the middle."

There were also other trade-offs that came with watching a movie at the drive-in. We were constantly reminded that we were essentially sitting outdoors on a hot summer night. And that meant mosquitoes. We tolerated a few, but at a certain point it became obvious that it was time for Dad to roll up the windows. That meant that instead of a nice breeze occasionally moving through the car, we sat in a stuffy sedan, all of us inhaling and exhaling in close quarters. This led to more complaints from the back seat. "Mom, she's breathing on me."

We tolerated the hotter and stuffier environment only until the windows started to fog up, at which point it was once again time to let in the fresh air and mosquitoes. Automobiles built in 1941 were not known for their advanced climate control, so this ritual went on pretty much all evening. A few families brought lawn chairs which they positioned directly in front of their cars, and at first, I thought that looked kind of fun. But watching them swat mosquitoes made me glad to be crammed into an enclosed space.

My sister and I were never big fans of movies that had a lot of kissing. Whenever there'd be a kissing scene, we covered our eyes and moaned, "Eeoooww!" If you wanted to see kissing, you could always just look in the car parked next to us. The young couple to our left had apparently decided that they were less interested in the movie than in each other. Happily, *The Long, Long Trailer* didn't have much kissing. It was mostly slapstick comedy interspersed with frequent arguments between the newly-weds which, come to think of it, was also quite funny.

The only thing more dreaded than the occasional kissing scene was the sudden appearance of a raindrop on our windshield. All too often, it would be followed by another. Then another. Then a sprinkling of drops that made us once again aware that we were sitting in a car parked out in a field. Usually, we sat half-watching the movie, and half-holding our breath, hoping the rain would stop. Occasionally, it did. But once in a while it became too difficult to see, and Dad had to turn on the windshield wipers, causing streaky smears that usually made it even harder to see. Automobiles of 1941 were also not noted for their high-tech power accessories. For one thing, the engine had to be running for the wipers to work. The wipers which ran off the vacuum of the engine consisted of short, flimsy arms that chattered in fits and starts, dragging the rain from one side to the other in little arcs across our field of vision, making it difficult to tell if Desi Arnaz was kissing Lucille Ball or blowing up a balloon. Seeing little point in the plot for the sudden appearance of a balloon, my sister and I concluded that it was probably another kissing scene, and though we couldn't see it very well, covered our eyes just to be safe.

Every once in a while the rain tapered off and Dad would turn off the wipers to see how long we could go before more smearing was necessary. Sometimes it rained so steadily that we'd see a few convertible tops stretch slowly up into the air before collapsing down to be snugly fastened, and some cars actually started to leave in the middle of the movie. Most drivers who had chosen to exit the theater politely turned on only their parking lights so as not to disturb other patrons. The people in the car next to us didn't seem to mind the rain. They were still kissing.

As often happens in mid-summer, the duration of passing showers can be brief. Families who decided to stay and take their chances were rewarded by getting to see the rest of the movie. They also got to experience something else of noteworthy entertainment value. Intermission. This respite from the feature presentation was marked by a heightened energy and excitement as a variety of animated snack foods sang and danced across the screen. Cartoon characters of hotdogs and popcorn were depicted in bright colors and the volume of the sound suddenly seemed to get louder.

Intermission was the time during which the theater operators did everything in their power to get moviegoers to respond to poorly executed, yet curiously enticing snack ads. Overdone hamburgers on pasty-white buns were filmed under lights so bright they looked like they were being interrogated. What was described by the announcer as "refreshing, icy-cold soft drinks" looked like warm ink sitting in paper cups. Yet, somehow, everyone got hungry. Maybe it was the way the announcer described the food, using phrases like, "piping hot pizza and mouth-watering, tasty snacks at our refreshment stand." Maybe it was seeing other people carrying armloads of great-smelling food back to their cars. Whatever the reason, people headed for the snack bar in droves, and Lucille and Desi would have to suffer the interruption while everyone took a break to get something to eat.

Mom always saved money by packing snacks from home. The drawback to this was that we didn't get to partake of the "frosty-cold ice cream bars in three flavors" or the "plump and juicy hotdogs grilled to perfection with all the fixin's." The benefit, of course, was that we didn't have to wait for intermission to start eating. By the time everyone else began heading to the concession stand to wait in long lines with other hungry families, we were already opening our second bag of cookies.

Even the intermission was interrupted. Every so often, an animated numeral would appear on the screen and a voice would announce with eager anticipation, "eight minutes 'til showtime," followed by a countdown of "five minutes 'til showtime," and so on. Even after Lucy and Desi had been back on the screen for several minutes, the movie's soundtrack was interrupted by the theater manager's loud voice warning, "The snack bar will be closing in ten minutes. Only ten minutes to enjoy..." He probably would have gone on to list all the food that they had left over had he not been chased off the intercom by the sound of honking car horns.

The rest of *The Long, Long Trailer* was just as funny as the first part. When their car got stuck on a dirt road in the middle of a rainstorm, Desi Arnaz tried to push it out, becoming covered with mud from the spinning tires. We all laughed so hard that our whole car started shaking. We could hear people all over the drive-in laughing in their cars, making us suddenly aware once again that we weren't alone, but were sitting out in the middle of a field with a hundred other cars all strangely facing in the same direction like students in a classroom.

By the end of the movie, I was struggling to keep my eyes open. I vaguely recall a mad scramble of cars all heading for two narrow exit lanes. The same man's voice that had interrupted to tell us that the snack bar was closing came on with one last announcement asking that drivers please replace their speakers on the posts before leaving the theater. My father obediently did so and we slowly inched out of our parking slot. The couple in the car next to us, I noticed, had not yet replaced their speaker, and were still kissing.

By the time we arrived home and pulled into our driveway, I was barely awake, but pretended to be fully asleep in order to be carried from the car up to my room. There was nothing in the world that felt better than already being in my pajamas, knowing that I didn't have to get ready for bed, and that I would be forgiven for not brushing my teeth until the morning.

Tonight, the feeling of my head gently sinking into the pillow was more comfortable than anything I could imagine. It was like floating off into space. Glorious, blissful space. Tonight, beautiful and happy images would fill my dreams, and I would not stir until morning. Tonight, I would not be going to the window to watch the slow parade of cars go by.

Driving Miss Daisy Crazy

Let me say at the outset that, while I do not hold myself guiltless of the events that transpired during the school year of 1963, it would be inappropriate to single out one individual for blame. A kind of cooperative insubordination swept over the group when the classroom door opened and Mrs. Nylander announced herself as the day's substitute teacher. As she turned to the blackboard to sign her name in perfect Palmer Method penmanship, she might as well have been writing, "Let the anarchy begin."

To everyone in my tenth-grade class, the appearance of Mrs. Nylander signalled a welcome break from the routine. An elderly, Jessica Tandy type, Mrs. Nylander was a sweet and obviously highly intelligent woman whose academic credentials were impeccable, but whose control over the class was utterly nonexistent. Her wireframe bifocals and greyish hair carefully arranged in a tidy bun became familiar omens of our good fortune. Her occasional stints as replacement instructor occurred on a semi-regular basis, and we knew her appearance meant that our lack of preparation for the day's lesson would remain undetected. For it was

Mrs. Nylander's customary practice to call upon only those students who voluntarily raised their hands. It was upon these goody-two-shoes that she also relied to apprise her of the day's current assignment.

Anyone who sat mute was excused from class participation with apparently no judgement. To call upon an unprepared student would subject her to wisecracks, backtalk, and contagious laughter with which she was ill-equipped to cope. It was clearly evident that she took no note of which students were well-prepared and which had not bothered even to bring their books to class. Except for a few individuals whom she happened to know personally, students retained their anonymity.

In addition to an academic reprieve—a day's free pass for incomplete homework—the presence of someone renowned for her lack of discipline was also a license for group misbehavior of the highest order. First or second graders might have seen her as a kindly, grandmother type and happily listened to a storybook reading or a lesson in simple arithmetic. But high school students intent on testing her lenient boundaries were another story. During her classes, the task of learning was temporarily suspended, her role effectively reduced to that of a glorified babysitter.

To say that we took advantage of Mrs. Nylander's good nature would be an understatement, and I do not exclude myself from the collective "we" that witnessed the transformation of our sophomore history class into an enthusiastic mini-rebellion. Although I was more a follower than a leader, ultimately, everyone participated to a certain extent in the insurgency. Even the brainy Edward Boyden suspended his role as class genius long enough to partake in the festivities.

The disturbances were never of a malicious nature. Most were simple annoyances. Howie Saaristo would typically incite the uprising by deliberately shuffling his chair. Not blatantly, but enough to produce an abrasive grating sound of wooden legs on the tile floor—the furniture equivalent of fingernails on a blackboard. He would look to another willing participant to indicate that the noise was indeed deliberate, and before long, a cacophony of scuffing chairs throughout the room had drown out the frail voice of our good-natured substitute, still intent on impressing upon an indifferent audience the relevance of the Monroe Doctrine.

A variety of loud, funny, or disgusting noises was always a popular disturbance. Harmless, yet entirely disruptive. Over time, our repertoire grew to accommodate the particular specialties of some of the more talented individuals and the spontaneity of others whose bodily functions seemed to come alive in the presence of our substitute teacher. I found it endlessly fascinating to watch the wave of disruption consume an entire classroom in a matter of seconds with virtually no planned coordination whatsoever. Sometimes the phenomenon would begin unintentionally. Like the time Susan Ott had a coughing fit during class. It took only three or four seconds for the remainder of the class to mimic her with deliberate and emphatic clearing of our throats in unison. It was in this way that reluctant participants were not only included in the event, but occasionally became its unwitting instigators. This seemed a relatively safe practice for which there would be no punitive action. No one would fault you for coughing in class. Least of all, Mrs. Nylander.

But the mere imitation of such commonplace sounds fell far short of what we knew we were capable of. This aspiration to a more fulfilling expression of our creativity eventually gave rise to what became known as jungle music. Andy Caless would always begin. Andy did the best monkey sounds in the entire tenth grade. Of course, the fact that he had been kept back in elementary school had given him a whole extra year to hone his skills. Students saw Andy's monkey sounds as both an invitation and a challenge. One by one, as apprehension faded, other wild animals would join the clamor until a bestial chorus emanated from all corners of the classroom. Elephants, lions, snorting pigs, gorillas, and all manner of exotic, screeching birds noisily announced their presence. This also gave us a chance to practice our ventriloquy skills, as the jungle sounds often continued for some time even after Mrs. Nylander had looked up from her lesson book. Many of us became quite proficient at imitating the sounds of animals without the slightest telltale movement of our lips.

Jungle music was my personal favorite of all our disruptions. It was so joyously raucous that it was difficult to keep the sounds from escalating into riotous laughter. I was amazed that Mrs. Nylander was able to continue teaching, apparently unaffected by such exuberant clamor. But years of practice had allowed her to remain apparently unflustered in the face of such an adolescent display of immaturity. Once in a great while she would politely ask us to settle down, and relative quiet would ensue, if only temporarily. That was the closest she ever got to showing any sign of irritation.

Once, the noise was so loud that Mr. Sullivan, who was teaching in the adjoining classroom, came in to ask if everything was alright. Seeing that Mrs. Nylander was clearly in over her head, he stayed for several minutes regaling us with a heartfelt discourse on the merits of common courtesy before retreating through the adjoining door to his own class which was itself beginning to show signs of unsupervised behavior. After his intrusion, the class remained relatively quiet for some time, as Mr. Sullivan had left the door separating the two classrooms slightly ajar. It wasn't until Wayne Decker fell backward in his chair that once again the class erupted into uncontrolled laughter.

Another intended irritant was a game we called foot hockey, though the fact that Mrs. Nylander seemed to not even notice greatly diminished the satisfaction of playing it. A sheet of paper that had been crumpled into a ball was passed from under one student's desk to another by means of inconspicuous footplay. Whenever Mrs. Nylander looked up from her textbook the game would stop, only to resume when she returned her attention to the lesson. Play was also temporarily halted if the paper ball landed at the feet of a reluctant participant. In such cases, all attention was focused on the uncooperative player until the pressure of such concentrated attention grew unbearable and the paper ball was again put into play. There was no goal, no points, and no teams. The object of the game was simply to keep the ball moving. If the ball became irretrievably lost in an inaccessible part of the room, it was considered a dead ball and another sheet of paper was crumpled up and put into play.

Occasionally, by the end of one of Mrs. Nylander's classes, the floor would be strewn with wadded-up paper. When the bell rang, dismissing the class, she always seemed baffled by the sudden accumulation of litter that had materialized around her desk. She always singled out the star player (usually John Veleno) as he bolted for the door to politely request that he pick up the paper balls and place them in the receptacle beside her desk before moving on to his next class. Her ability to somehow identify the lead culprit was uncanny, since it seemed she had little, if any, awareness of the play while it was occurring. Relieved that he was not being reprimanded or even accused, John politely obliged with a slightly embarrassed look that seemed to convey an unspoken apology.

Charlie Liebfried stumbled upon an idea one afternoon that provided an entertaining, though shortlived distraction during one of Mrs. Nylander's classes. Every day after lunch, the sunlight streamed through the windows on the south side of the school building and bathed those class-rooms in bright, glaring light. For students sitting nearest the windows, it provided a lazy warmth conducive to day-dreaming that was especially welcome after two Sloppy Joes and an ice cream sandwich. On one such afternoon, quite by accident, the face of Charlie's wristwatch caught the direct sunlight at such an angle that a perfect circle of light was cast onto the blackboard where Mrs. Nylander was busy conjugating French verbs. The slightest movement of his arm caused the bright circle to dance wildly, and he found that he could control the reflection to such an extent that not only was it extremely annoying for Mrs. Nylander as she was writing, but it was almost impossible to detect its origin. Each time she turned around, everyone would be intently following along in their textbooks or diligently taking notes. When Mrs. Nylander once again turned her back, a nearly imperceptible movement of Charlie's wrist caused the annoying spot to reappear in front of her.

It occurred to me that by meticulously cutting tiny let-ters out of masking tape, and applying them to the face of a watch, it might be possible to spell out simple messages with the projected image. Nothing complicated. Something like "Hi" or "Wow" would be quite enough to distract the atten-tion of the class from the lessons at hand. I never got the chance to conduct my little physics experiment, however. Mrs. Nylander turned from the board, and with arms crossed around her thick copy of *Adventures in French*, walked slowly over to the sunny side of the classroom and paced the length of the row of desks along the bank of windows. I thought how uncharacteristic it would be if she were to confront a student or even dare to ask what might be causing the reflection. Reaching the back of the room, she turned and slowly retraced her steps, tapping her fingers impatiently on her textbook. Then, stopping directly in front of Charlie Liebfried's desk, she put an abrupt and immediate end to the entire situation. She looked Charlie squarely in the eye, raised one arm above her head, and with one emphatic gesture, pulled the cord that drew the blinds closed.

She actually made poor Charlie flinch as he prepared to duck out of the way of a slap to the back of the head. I never saw Mrs. Nylander take control of a situation as completely and decisively as she had at that moment. And all without having said a single word. I was kind of proud of her that day for the calm and dignified way in which she had handled the situation. I think she was too, as she strode back to her desk wearing a self-satisfied victory smirk.

Despite our misbehavior, I felt sorry for Mrs. Nylander, though by today's standards, our harmless mischief was just that. These were not the days of drugs, metal detectors, and school shootings. The item most closely resembling a weapon I recall at my small, suburban high school was the day in chemistry lab when Alan Flood fashioned his Bunsen burner into a makeshift flamethrower with surprising, and I might add, breathtaking results.

And the closest thing to a school shooting ever reported at my alma mater were the spitballs fired through cut-off drinking straws, often with stinging accuracy. Rather than hitting the blackboard, an easier and more benign target, the soggy projectiles often found their mark on the back of someone's neck, causing the receiver to wince and emit an audible "yeoow!" I would happily have done without the presence of spitballs. Any object propelled at high velocity and consisting largely of bodily fluids is just not my idea of hygienically conducive entertainment.

By comparison to current trends, these were distinctly more innocent times. During my years in high school, about the worst fate that could befall a student was to be caught smoking in the boys' room. I don't mean smoking a joint. We had barely even heard of marijuana. I'm talking about Chesterfields and Pall Malls. And even at that, the students who flaunted their colorful packs of smokes were limited to an undesirable few. School authorities knew them as juvenile delinquents, or JDs. In my school we called them "ruggies," a derivation, I believe, of the word rugged and, no doubt, a somewhat regional colloquialism. Ruggies could be easily identified by their black leather jackets, turned-up collars, long sideburns, slouched posture, and practiced looks of sinister intent. Another outstanding feature of the genre was their greased-back hair that was somehow coaxed into twirls and flips of the most graceful artforms. Even if I had had the disposition and the nerve for pursuing a life of troublemaking, I could never have been a juvenile delinquent. I didn't have the hair for it.

Ruggies were rarely seen on those big, yellow clown vehicles known as school busses, preferring instead to drive their own cars—low-riding sedans that had been decked out with after-market accessories designed to command maximum attention. Most of their cars were coated in dull-gray primer, anticipating an undisclosed time in the future when they would presumably be given a proper paint job.

In addition to fuzzy dice and fender skirts, these cars were often equipped with glasspacks—loud mufflers packed with fiberglass that produced quite an intimidating sound after being given enough gas and then letting up on the accelerator pedal. It was all part of the whole tough-guy image. I once made the mistake of telling one of the ruggies that his car sounded like a really loud whoopie cushion. He unceremoniously dumped my books on the ground just before climbing into his souped-up '52 Mercury and taking off with the school slut. I guess I showed him.

In striking testimony to their committed indifference to education, many of the ruggies were older than those of us in the same grade. Dave Larkin had been held back so often that by sixth-period English class he had a five o'clock shadow. It's rumored that one day during junior year, he was excused from gym class so he could be allowed to go vote.

These, however, were not the students who harassed our dear Mrs. Nylander. To someone who boasted of having his own probation officer, misbehaving in class was kids' stuff. These were the students who, when they learned a substitute teacher was taking over the class, didn't even bother showing up, but instead, headed directly for their cars. Through the classroom windows we could hear them announce their premature departure with the prolonged sound of screeching tires. By the end of the school year, they had substantially completed the task of generously repaving the far end of the school parking lot with rubber.

It was just as well that these hoodlums saw fit to skip Mrs. Nylander's classes. Their unwelcome presence could easily have turned our innocent pranks into large-scale events resulting in fire alarms and school evacuations. Though you'd not have guessed it from my behavior, I rather liked Mrs. Nylander and I would not have wanted her subjected to such seasoned troublemakers.

Amid the annoying noises, rubber band shooting, and other largely innocent disruptions designed to distract her, Mrs. Nylander kept right on teaching, ignoring the commotion that went on right under her nose. It was clear that she loved teaching, and was as comfortable instructing us in French as she was in history or English, despite our best efforts to keep her from doing so. But the fact that she remained unperturbed by our constant attempts at annoyance did not go unnoticed. And the fact that she never stopped trying to teach us made a profound impression on me, though apparently not enough to inspire me to learn.

So what is it, after forty-some-odd years, that causes an obscure substitute teacher to remain so prominent in my awareness? Is it the vast education I received as a result of her dedication? Is it the great appreciation she instilled in me for French literature? Or the nagging guilt I still feel after all these decades? ... Nah.

In the intervening years, few occasions have required me to recall the major battles of the Civil War. And even the most basic French phrases now elude me. Mrs. Nylander wasn't teaching us history. Nor was she teaching us French or English. Looking back on her tutelage, I now see that without even realizing that I had learned it, I have put into practice a more valuable and relevant lesson. It was a lesson found in no textbook. There was no final exam. It was a subliminal lesson taught by example, and inexplicably learned through osmosis, though it is unlikely that Mrs. Nylander could have imagined the extent to which it would impact me.

Through the nearly constant disruption, indeed, *because* of it, Mrs. Nylander was able to demonstrate what it means to live in harmony and without conflict. As a striking exemplar of this principle, she rarely even acknowledged our misbehavior, thus defusing it in the most effective way possible. She never stooped to our level, and never reinforced our misconduct with confrontation. For the most part, she remained above the fray, totally ignoring our attempts at disruption. That not only took most of the fun out of it, but would usually cause troublemakers to eventually stop of their own accord, having received little reaction to show for their efforts. This non-action is implicit in the phrase, "What we resist persists."

As a so-called adult, I now practice the teaching that Mrs. Nylander constantly demonstrated merely by being herself. It is the only lesson learned in school that I can truly say I use every day. Today, there are few things in life that bother me. I am not distracted by petty incidents that happen and will always continue to happen. I have learned that the quality of our lives is not determined by what happens around us, but by how we respond to it. It is a lesson I will always remember. And its teacher, I will never forget.

Barbara Nylander passed away in 2002 after a lifetime of dedicated service to teaching. While it may be said that she lived to teach, it must also be remembered that she taught how to live.

MAD-ly Mistaken

During the thirteen years in which my presence had graced the planet, few trips to the mailbox had caused such exuberant anticipation. I ran home at top speed wanting to scream with delight, but my adolescent voice, still in the process of changing, was capable only of cackling sounds more suggestive of torture. My excitement reached its peak as I flung wide the screen door and burst into the house, spilling an armload of bills and flyers onto the kitchen table and tearing into the only piece of mail that had any real importance.

The return address indicated that the letter had originated in New York City, and had come in response to articles I had submitted in hopes of having them published by a magazine that I held in the highest esteem. I unfolded the single-sided letter, immediately noting that it was not a generic, typed document, but a personalized correspondence penned by hand on the official letterhead of the editor himself. My work must have really impressed them, I thought, to generate a response from someone so important. Surely, words of encouragement such as this do not come along every day. The gradual realization that what I was reading was a rejection letter did little to diminish my excitement. For the first time in my young life, a world-renowned publication had taken note of my creative writing, and had considered it worthy enough to merit a response. The thrill of having been acknowledged for my work would inspire me to persevere.

My rejection did not come from what I considered to be some stodgy, uninspired periodical such as *The New Yorker* magazine, a rather commonplace occurrence that must happen dozens of time each day by impersonal form letter. Nor was it a rebuff by a frivolous, kids' publication like *The Weekly Reader.* On the contrary, my submissions were rejected by a publication that I considered to be on the forefront of cutting edge journalism—the holy grail of social commentary, cunning satire, and unmatched wit. An institution that I held in such high regard that I considered its personalized rejection of my work to be an honor that, for several years to come, would be the crowning achievement of my budding life.

Receiving my rejection letter from *Mad Magazine* was like being turned down for a date by Annette Funicello. It was a slap in the face that felt great. I knew it was a long shot. Chances were probably greater that I would be drafted by the Boston Red Sox right out of junior high. But the very fact that I had been personally acknowledged by people that I held in such high regard was, for me, the ultimate praise. The top of the letterhead was emblazoned with the iconic "Mad" lettering that I attempted to emulate whenever I was bored enough to doodle in class (which was most of the time). Next to that was a picture of a face familiar to readers all over the country—none other than Alfred E. Newman himself. Below his smiling caricature was the famous motto, *"What—Me worry?"* I carried the letter around for weeks showing it to whomever I thought would be suitably impressed. I was certain that my work had so impressed the editors at *Mad Magazine* that they had felt compelled to drop whatever they were doing and draft an immediate response.

I theorized that, legally, they had little choice but to issue my polite, but reluctant rejection. I rationalized that, of course, it had nothing to do with the actual quality of my submissions, but rather only my young age. I bragged to my friends that being a minor and barely in my teens, the reluctance of the publication to run my articles undoubtedly had to do with child labor laws or something like that. I reminded them of what we had read in history class about children working in the textile mills in the early 1900s, and how because of their mistreatment, it was now nearly impossible for any big corporation to hire a kid. My classmates politely nodded as I crafted my explanation. I took this as confirmation of my logical assumption.

"A big company like that couldn't just write you a check and publish your work," my know-it-all friend, Eddie, interjected in his unusually loud voice. "My dad's a lawyer," he boasted, "and he knows all about this stuff. You'd probably need to fill out all sorts of legal contracts and get an out-of-state work permit. Then there are tax laws that you'd have to deal with. It's all pretty complicated," he added, confidently displaying his intimate knowledge of corporate law.

"It's obvious," I agreed, "that their hands were tied and that they are legally prevented from paying me huge sums of money for my work because I'm under age. I'm quite certain," I continued, "that the government has laws that prevent kids like me from taking good jobs away from grown-ups who need the money more."

When I showed the letter to my eleven-year-old friend, Kenny, he asked me, "Why didn't they just come right out and say that?"

"Well," I answered, looking over my oversized glasses at him. "It's kind of a grown-up thing. You'll understand when you're older like me. Adults in business often don't say exactly what they really mean. That way they don't get sued."

I explained to him that I didn't hold it against them because I was sure that everyone at *Mad* must have been quite impressed by my sharp wit and clever illustrations. It could not have been otherwise. Oh, they hadn't come right out and said as much. But I could read between the lines. If they hadn't thought so much of my work, they wouldn't have encouraged me like this. They would have simply ignored it, or at the very most, had some secretary send me a terse note. But my letter came straight from Jerry DeFuccio himself. His name was listed right on the inside cover of every issue of *Mad Magazine*. I mean, he was practically famous.

"And look at this!" I continued. "He signed my letter with the word 'MAD-ly.' That must be like a secret handshake or something. Otherwise he would have simply written, 'sincerely,' or 'yours truly.' But he didn't. He said, 'MAD-ly.' It's as if he's saying I'm one of them. Like a member of an exclusive club."

But Kenny wasn't buying any of this. He left on his bike, shaking his head and sending loose gravel flying up in my direction.

"Hmphh," I snorted. "Kids."

My grandmother, on the other hand, had shown what I felt was the proper measure of enthusiasm for my rejection. On the night I showed her my letter, she served me what I perceived to be an extra large portion of dessert, although I wasn't sure she had ever heard of *Mad Magazine*. She kept asking me, "what's the name of the magazine again?" Then, she'd repeatedly ask why they gave it such a silly name.

I felt that my English teacher also had shown me an appropriate degree of support. She told me she had been impressed by my initiative, then went on to add that if I kept writing, one day I might be lucky enough to have my work rejected by a *real* publication. Despite her encouragement, I kept writing and illustrating anyway.

For years, I kept the letter folded neatly in a shoebox under my bed along with a baseball signed by Ted Williams,

a collection of shell casings from real bullets, and a rattle
that my uncle told me he'd severed with a jackknife from
the tail of a live rattlesnake. The *Mad* letter became a familiar icon of my teenage years, and on occasion I slid the
shoebox out from under my bed to reread the words
scrawled in bold blue ink. I rewrote the letter countless
times in my mind, attempting to paraphrase what the editor
of my favorite literary publication really had meant to say,
but had been unable to find the exact words. *We'd love to
pay you a lot of money for your great work, but some of our best
writers have trouble coming up with ideas, and they'd be very
jealous if they knew a boy of thirteen was capable of this kind of
genius.*

It never occurred to me that my ideas might not be
compelling enough to merit publishing, even though they
might have benefitted from a little tweaking. I was certainly not averse to having the editors at *Mad* make a few small
changes, although I failed to see how my ideas might have
been improved. I wondered if perhaps I should have men-
tioned this fact in the letter that I had sent along with my
submissions, and I considered writing again to make sure
they understood that, if they wanted, they could make a few
tiny revisions. Ultimately, I decided that they probably
already understood this, and I would simply wait for them to
change their minds and reconsider publishing my work. I
envisioned my layouts pinned to a bulletin board in their
big New York City offices where one day someone would
walk in and see them and say, "Wow, these articles are

great! Why aren't you running these?" I pictured myself in my own office at their Manhattan headquarters where co-workers would introduce me as "the youngest employee to ever work at *Mad Magazine*." I imagined it would be a really fun place to work where everyone was always joking around and laughing. I could hardly wait to apply for a job with them, although they'd probably make me wait until I had graduated from high school.

Alas, countless issues were subsequently published, and each time, without the inclusion of my work. At the very least, I thought they might eventually write to ask me if I had any more ideas for articles. Somewhere around the age of sixteen I decided that they were probably not going to call me back and admit their poor judgement in the hasty dismissal of my work.

In 2001, when I learned that Jerry DeFuccio had passed away, I dug out the letter he had written so many years before. In reading it for the first time in decades, I was astonished to find no mention of how great my work was. There was nothing about child labor laws preventing them from paying me for my ideas. I sensed no unexpressed thoughts between the hurriedly scribbled lines encouraging me to keep writing, and to resubmit more ideas as I created them. There was no evidence of the praise that I had remembered and built up in my mind. Not even a "thank you." In fact, it seemed a rather curt note dashed off merely to placate a paying subscriber. Reading it in the cold light of day, they were definitely brushing me off. Giving me the bum's rush.

I began to wonder if they had even bothered to look at my ideas, or whether they had thrown them in the trash before recognizing the potential of what I had submitted. The instant they saw that I was only a kid, they probably dismissed me out of hand, thinking that no thirteen-year-old could possibly have any ideas worth looking at. "Hmphh! Grown-ups."

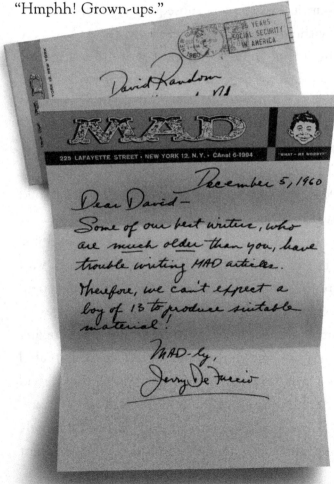

Straight From
My Friend's Mouth

My young friend, Josh, approached me one morning to proudly demonstrate his prowess at burping the alphabet. He duly noted that "W" had a high degree of difficulty, while vowels, particularly "O" and "E," aside from their ease of performance, yielded an especially resonant quality, to which I will readily attest. He also noted that the quantity of intake bore a direct correlation to the quality of outflow.

While being mindful not to overly praise such vocal dexterity, it occurred to me that the degree of analysis to which he had taken the art deserved at least a modicum of recognition. It wasn't his breath control, or his skillful enunciation so much as the fact that he had methodically examined subtle acoustic differences that impressed me. For a second grader to have differentiated between the open-mouthed vowels and the more clipped consonants as a criteria for having developed favorites was not only observant, but demonstrated a thoughtfulness that went beyond his aptitude for distasteful noises.

While not necessarily a skill whose practiced performance would put him in good stead during, say, a job interview, I thought such analytical skills, properly channeled, might prove useful tools in later life. For a seven-year-old to apply such principles of scientific discipline to an activity that one might easily take merely at face value was impressive, to say the least.

I inquired about other noteworthy characteristics he might have observed and discovered that he was not alone in his talent. Two other boys in his classroom had apparently been gifted with similar innate abilities. Based on the burp language, the three had formed a club whose sole criteria for admission was the ability to inhale gulps of air and then expel them on demand while speaking.

After discussing how envious his other classmates must be for his having developed this acumen at such an early age, I was treated to a further dissertation of oral skill for which words fail me. As Josh began burping out complete sentences, remarking on the discipline necessary to perform such a recital, I found myself secretly wondering where such fascination might lead.

Recalling my own preoccupation with bodily noises at that age, it occurred to me that such curiosity and experimentation is not something to which adults readily aspire. Rather, these are qualities born and developed at a young age, practiced through childhood, and honed in adolescence. But these activities are not without virtue. The principles of physics and acoustics as applied to the grosser forms of anatomical functions have a certain relevance in the technological advancement of our society. Regardless of the form in which the laws of matter and energy are demonstrated, it is the awareness of these principles upon which every new generation contributes to our collective progress.

It is within the realm of possibility that little Albert Einstein planted the seeds of his theory of relativity while noticing the failure of farts to smell while riding his bike at high speed. And perhaps a toddling Charlie Darwin developed his life-long fascination with the multitudinous yet subtle variations of life-forms while picking his nose. Even medical advances in sound therapy and vibrational healing probably began when someone noticed how good it felt to make certain noises. I cannot deny that, since early childhood, I have derived pleasure from vocal experimentation and the baser forms of bodily acoustics when I thought no one else could hear me.

Josh placed his elbows on the edge of my desk and leaned in close to me as he finished his guttural chorus with a multi-syllabic crescendo. Is this, I thought, the next Sir Isaac Newton? Could this be a Michael Faraday or Marconi in the making? I studied his face for signs of thoughtful epiphany. Were the wheels of perception turning behind that impish grin?

When it became clear to Josh that his rendition had not garnered the intended response on my part, he summoned forth a prolonged, throaty pronouncement. As he ran laughing into the next room hoping to illicit a more appropriate response from someone closer to his own age, I knew at once I had the answer to my query. Was I witnessing an awareness from which would spring tomorrow's theories of quantum mechanics?

Nope. It's just my little friend, Josh, making disgusting noises.

The Family Soup Recipe that Made Me Blind

I can't remember exactly when I became aware that my family was the apparent guardian of this extraordinary secret. But I knew at an early age it was something special. None of my fellow second graders had ever heard of the strange, fist-shaped balls which I described as they listened with appropriate awe and envy.

And such a curious name—klössens. I carefully pronounced the word for my friends so they would take proper notice. "Klay´-shuns." Why, the very word held such mystique. Never had I heard the syllables uttered outside of my immediate family. A fact of which I took full advantage. Growing up in small-town Massachusetts, your opportunities to dazzle classmates with such impressive vocabulary were pretty limited. Small wonder that it peppered my usual kidspeak on a regular basis.

And what of the sacred objects themselves? Klössens. I'd chase them around the bottom of my soup bowl like slippery, sunken treasure, where they'd usually evade several advances before finally succumbing to my skillful spoonmanship. Cutting them in half, then in half again, was tricky, but the only way to fit the careful prize into my seven-year-old mouth. My young modesty prevented me from calling attention to my obvious mastery of such a delicate maneuver. But I took secret delight in being able to so adeptly control the elusive little dumplings.

So how did it come to pass that my family was singled out to possess the secret of the klössen? A secret to be handed down mother to daughter, generation after generation. It would seem unlikely that we were to be its sole heirs. But to my knowledge, no family member had ever questioned the source of this birthright. It's origin was never spoken of. No one knew the identity of the wizard or sorcerer who, generations ago, must have bestowed upon our distant ancestors the solemn charge which we were to carry forth for future soup archeologists to one day discover. We only knew that when we heard the clank of the ladle and the words "klössen soup" that we were in for a special treat.

After nearly filling our bowls with the chicken and vegetable broth, we would ration, one by one, the slippery shapes with the funny, but oh so familiar name. We were mindful not to exceed our allotted number of the precious dumplings—three or four, I don't recall. But I do remember the biggest ones were always the first to be claimed as we hunted them down in the steamy depths of the great pot. Occasionally, I can remember scooping into my bowl a particularly small klössen, hoping that it would slip uncounted beneath the glistening surface of the broth where it would elude the sideways gaze of my spoonmates.

Such was my small part in helping to ensure that such important knowledge was not lost to history. It was a duty we gladly accepted. For it would have been a betrayal of our responsibility to have squandered this confidence for future generations by allowing it to slip forgotten into the past. It would have been unforgivable had this knowledge been allowed to go the way of some ancient language whose speakers, through its disuse, had forced it to revert to meaningless symbols.

It wasn't until years later when, as a young adult describing the dense, little delicacies to an acquaintance, he responded, "Oh! Matzah balls."

"No, these are different," I started to say. "These are…"

But the words would not come. I felt them filling my mouth to overfull, but they were somehow disconnected from my thoughts. Thoughts that were swimming in a terrible swirl of confusion. I felt a sort of bubble bursting around me. No, not bursting really. More like deflating. And slowly. It didn't happen in an instant as I recall. It took several minutes to dispel the swell of denial that rose up in response to this new crack in the foundation of my core beliefs. It felt, I supposed, like the moment at which I realized there was no Santa Claus. But why should it matter? Nothing had changed. Certainly not the klössens. They were real. The great pot. The ladle. The counting. The cutting. All real. Nothing had changed.

But, somehow *everything* had changed. No longer was there an ancient birthright which ensured our distinction among more common families. No longer was there a culinary secret known only to us and a few privileged individuals of antiquity. Individuals who, in their infinite wisdom, had locked a secret away with us until the world was ready. But the world *was* ready. It was never *not* ready. And it had a name for our very own private tradition—Matzah Ball Soup.

What my family had was not some ancient privity. What my family had was a word. A funny-sounding word which my German ancestors had carried with them to a strange, new world where it was to become a comforting reminder of warm kitchens back home. But once here, it was to become much more than a word. Here, it was to take on a life of its own.

My ancestors could not have foreseen just how big this klössen thing would become to an impressionable, young boy. This enviable knowledge was to become a talisman. An emotional touchstone. A defining difference. Yet how could I have been so blind to the truth hiding behind the word? Was it possible that everyone was in on the joke but me? Was I too busy as a child consuming the little dumplings and, in turn, being consumed by their mystique? Had I missed the wink of the eye?

But that was decades ago, and the trauma is nearly passed. The soup ritual is still tradition in my family. The klössens are still lovingly formed by practiced hands. The meal is yet a special event to be savored until the last leftover is consumed. An event remembered with fondness by grandchildren until once again the great pot is warmed from its dormant cupboard with great anticipation.

These days, however, the strict rationing has been replaced with a more polite restraint. Or could it be that the klössen has lost some of its mystique? Is it possible that because of knowing that the sturdy little balls reside in soup bowls the world over they now seem less special?

Regardless, we cannot bring ourselves to utter the blasphemy of their more common nomenclature. We cannot give up our old friends to a more indifferent world of soupdom. Tattered recipe cards are still faithfully copied by the daughters of daughters as "Klössen Soup." Sure, there are those little touches which make the recipe our own. Variations on a theme. Nothing more. They're still "you-know-what."

I'm Sorry, Mr. Grey Can't See You Now. He's Tied Up at the Moment.

I had always heard that the events that make the biggest impressions on us — the ones that create indelible memories — are often those that happen during our years in school. It seemed improbable at the time, that an event that came and went in the span of ten minutes would remain so vividly clear these many years later, but such is the unlikely case. What took place in those few minutes back at Acton-Boxboro Regional High School is as clear to me now as the day it happened.

In the intervening years, I have replayed in my mind every detail of that day when, using a coil of rope I had brought from home, I tied my high school principal, Mr. Grey, to the chair in his office. After making sure that he was securely bound in place, I took Polaroid pictures to document the event. It was one of my most memorable high school achievements.

"Pudgie," as he was aptly nicknamed, was a portly individual whose gruff voice more closely resembled a growl. Although he was shorter than a good many of the students over whom he presided, his larger-than-life presence was a constant reminder of his absolute authority.

Mr. Grey reveled in his position of power, and took every opportunity to bellow at students for the slightest slip. It would not have been unusual for him to single out a favorite target to bark at for some minor infraction of our questionable dress code.

"Mr. Berger, tuck in that shirt!" His booming voice would seem to come out of nowhere and make the hair on the back of your neck stand on end as you instinctively checked your own wardrobe.

Other favorite violations included needing a haircut, having your top two shirt buttons undone, or not having a book cover on one of your textbooks. He showed little deference toward female students and was just as apt to reprimand a young lady for a skirt that had been hemmed too high above the knee.

If Mr. Grey had a sense of humor, it was not a trait he readily displayed to students; I can remember few smiles ever to appear on his face, and even those seemed rather like sneers. Facial expressions of any kind, in fact, would cause his double chin to bulge, putting an enormous amount of stress on the collar of his shirt. Whenever Mr. Grey was angry (a state which seemed nearly perpetual), students in his immediate vicinity would hold their breath as they watched his quivering chins turn a deep scarlet red, and the shirt button at his throat threaten to pop like the bursting of a dam. The veins in his head often seemed nearly on the verge of exploding.

Tightly restraining Mr. Grey in his office chair, it seemed, would be the perfect act of defiance to symbolically mock his unquestioned authority. I considered it somewhat akin to poking a hornets' nest with a stick, but I ultimately determined that it would be worth any possible consequence.

As brazen as this scheme may sound, I must admit that this stunt was not something I planned to accomplish by casually popping into his office one day between algebra and science class. I would never have dared to put him in such a humiliating position when I was a student. Some fifteen years, in fact, would pass after my high school graduation before my insolent scheme would come to pass.

On the day my plan was to be carried out, I entered the school through a side door. Everything looked smaller than when I had attended classes here, and the deserted corridors felt strange. It was as if I had returned in a time machine to some far-off place of my distant youth. Yet a vague familiarity haunted me as I silently walked past classrooms full of bored-looking students and headed toward the administrative offices. I carried my rope in a large paper bag so as not to attract undue attention, although I passed no one as I walked unchallenged through the empty halls of my alma mater.

My graduating class—the class of '65—had left these premises without looking back. There had been no five-year, or ten-year reunions, no official contact of any kind since graduation. I had decided, along with three fellow classmates, however, not to allow this, the fifteenth year, to pass without a celebration in recognition of our final liberation from this memorable facility.

We were not class officers, and had no access to our class treasury, if indeed there was anything left after Charles Primiano, our class president, had seen fit to spend lavishly on a senior banquet that none of us could even recall. There was nothing official about us, but we had decided to take matters into our own hands and mark the occasion with one extravagant and unforgettable reunion.

After tracking down as many of our classmates as possible, we planned to send out an invitation that would be so cleverly compelling that failing to show up at the reunion would be unthinkable. Mr. Grey would be the first invited guest. But not until after I had accomplished my mission here today.

As I approached Mr. Grey's office, I could feel my heart pounding faster. Fifteen years after I had last heard his booming voice shake these corridors, I could still hear its echo rattling the doors of the metal lockers. I could hear his raspy growl as he reprimanded students for loitering in the halls. The thought of it still gave me pause, but I knew there would be no turning back, and I clutched my brown paper bag tightly as I marched on with stubborn resolve. I had come this far, and I would not abandon my plan.

At last the doorway loomed up in front of me. A small brass sign on the adjacent wall read, *Raymond J. Grey – Superintendent of Schools.* In the fifteen years that had passed since graduation, Mr. Grey had replaced his former boss, Mr. O'Connell, in his ascent from principal to the exalted role of Superintendent, a lofty position from which he could wield even greater power.

I took a deep breath and stepped into the reception office, a rather sterile ante-room that acted as a buffer for those wishing to enter the inner sanctum. A demure woman of indeterminate age greeted me in a business-like manner.

"May I help you?" she asked, looking over the rim of her fashionable eyeglasses.

"Yes. I'm here to see Mr. Grey."

"I'm sorry, Mr. Grey's in a meeting," she informed me. "Do you have an appointment?"

"Well, no. But I just need to see him for a minute."

"Well, he probably won't be available for about half an hour," she responded with an apologetic look, eyeing my paper bag.

"That's okay. I'll wait," I said, taking one of the seats against the wall opposite her desk.

"Who shall I say is waiting?" she quizzed, pen in hand, about to write on the pad beside her phone.

"I'm a former student. But I want to surprise him."

She seemed to accept my response, as she returned the pen to a flowery holder on her desk and resumed her paperwork. I'm sure the surprise she pictured differed considerably from the one I had in mind. I sat politely, clutching the bag on my lap, gazing around the small room, remembering one occasion during my junior year when I had been sent to

Mr. Grey's office for punching another student. Aside from that unfortunate incident and a few quietly ineffectual student rebellions that I had attempted to instigate regarding the dress code, I had been a fairly compliant student. So much so, that on the particular occasion when I had been exiled to his office, Mr. Grey had dismissed me with no more than an uncharacteristic mild warning.

But I was now beyond the reach of school authorities. There would be no disciplinary action if what I was about to attempt did not meet with Mr. Grey's approval. What could he do, suspend me? This thought gave me some comfort until I realized that my actions, should he disapprove, would now, perhaps, be a matter for the local police.

Without lifting her head from her work, the receptionist again looked over her glasses at me. I drew my bag closer to me and continued to wait.

Not more than twenty minutes had passed when the door to Mr. Grey's inner office opened to allow a man about my age to exit. I assume the man was a teacher. He looked slightly frazzled, and wore a bow tie, which, if memory serves, was conventional dress for all math teachers. He was followed seconds later by the man himself—Mr. Grey. Pudgie.

Remarkably, he looked exactly the same as he had fifteen years prior. It was as if with each new school year, everyone in the building was destined to duplicate with exact precision the same drudgery of every year that had come before. Even his suit looked like the one I had last seen him wearing. After shaking hands with the man in the bow tie, he turned in my direction, and without the slightest trace of a smile, growled, "What can I do for you?" It was clear that Mr. Grey was not having a good day.

I introduced myself, explaining that I had attended the school some fifteen years earlier.

"Yes," he acknowledged, though I wasn't sure he actually remembered me. "What brings you back here?"

I looked him straight in the eye as I answered, as it was the only certain way to keep from staring at his chins that jiggled with every raspy word. I asked if I could accompany him into his office for a minute of his time. Without speaking, he turned toward his office and I followed his wide torso through the doorway, still tightly clutching the bag that held my rope. I was relieved when, sensing the need for privacy, he closed the door behind us. I would have felt conspicuous tying him to his chair in full view of his secretary. It would be strange enough doing this in private, but I steeled myself for the task at hand, and waited for him to sit down.

I had, perhaps, been remiss in not rehearsing in my mind what was about to happen. I had pictured the end result quite clearly—Mr. Grey completely and humiliatingly trussed to his seat of power—but not exactly how I would accomplish it, and I wondered how I should begin the process now that we were face to face. Should I just stand up and start tying? Should I politely ask him first if it would please be okay? Both seemed like good ways to find myself back out on the street. My mind was racing with scenarios that I should have thought about before hand. We sat for an uncomfortable moment as I wondered how to broach the subject and begin my prank, when Mr. Grey abruptly barked, "What's in the bag?"

Knowing that this was the perfect segue to my next inevitable move, I reached into my parcel and produced the coil of rope, which suddenly seemed embarrassingly inappropriate. I now found myself staring at his chins in an effort to avoid eye contact.

"Well, Mr. Grey," I began, talking directly to the fleshy bulge squeezing out from above his collar, "I had this idea that I hoped you might help me with."

I stood up and walked around to the other side of his desk and tied one end of the rope to the arm of his chair as I started to explain my plan. Talking and tying at the same time, I spoke in one long run-on sentence, barely taking a breath for fear he would interrupt me and ruin everything. I remember being more than a little surprised that he did not question me as I tied the first knot, apparently content to hear my explanation.

I immediately assured him that my intentions were all in good fun, and began walking around the chair, encircling him with the coils. I explained that the motive for my odd behavior was in anticipation of the upcoming fifteen-year reunion, and that his cooperation could help assure its success. I repeatedly drew the rope across his necktie in front, and then around to the back of his swivel chair. His bulky torso seemed to expand beyond the typical three dimensions of space, and now seemed to take on a heightened reality. It was as if I were awakening from a bizarre dream to discover that it was actually happening. That I was actually doing this in real life.

Since there had been so little interest to date in any sort of official get-together, I explained, my biggest concern was to make everyone aware of the event, and to get as many students as possible to attend. For this, I reasoned, I would need a picture of him constrained to his chair. He frowned skeptically, but, apparently willing to hear the rest of my explanation, allowed me to continue. Surprisingly, he did not resist the completion of my handiwork.

In retrospect, had I fully explained my intentions at the outset and then politely asked his permission, I can't say what he might have done. It's possible that he might have said, "Sure. Nothing would give me greater pleasure than to be tied up in a chair in my office." But given time to ponder the situation and the resulting photographs, he might simply have stared at me and growled, at which point I'd have lost my nerve, thanked him for his time, and quickly departed. Once denied permission to execute my plan, it would have then been too late to continue.

But by winding the rope around him as I explained my plan, by the time I had finished my elaborate explanation, he was pretty much already secured behind his desk. I had further explained that my need to photograph him in such a subservient position was for the purpose of creating a ransom note that would be sent to all of my classmates. The ransom note would be my compelling invitation to the big reunion. Using words ripped out of magazines, I would paste a message under his photo that would read simply, "WE HAVE A HOSTAGE. COME TO THE REUNION, OR KISS THE PRINCIPAL GOODBYE."

Mr. Grey's reaction surprised me. Instead of voicing his displeasure and gruffly ordering me out of his office, I think he might have actually smiled. It was hard to tell. He was tied up, and I was still staring at his chins. But in the pictures he let me take of him, there was kind of a twinkle in his eye. He looked like he might actually be getting a kick out of this whole thing, and I told him that we'd love to have him come to the reunion as our guest of honor. Feeling the tension abate, I attempted to throw in a little humor by adding that, if he accepted our invitation, I'd even untie him.

Mr. Grey did not laugh, and I took that as my cue that I had reached the limit of his amusement. After uncoiling the rope from around his chest, we chatted for another minute or so, remembering others who had been in my class. He informed me that he'd be delighted to attend the reunion, which was scheduled to take place in about two months. As I turned to leave the office, his last words to me were, "Better keep that rope in the bag. We don't want anyone to get the wrong idea." His voice sounded friendly. Not like a growl at all.

In the summer of that year, a gratifying number of classmates showed up to reconnect and reminisce about our years under the tyrannical rule of our former principal. The reunion was a huge success, despite the fact that Mr. Grey was not in attendance. He died of a massive heart attack shortly after I made my unannounced visit to his office. The photos documenting our meeting that day were the last ever taken of him, and the words I had pasted under his picture became suddenly prophetic.

I decided, however, not to abandon my plan, and to send the invitations anyway. I considered it a way of honoring a man whose lighter side had finally emerged after so many years. I thought if this photo could help my classmates look beyond all the bravado, and see a warm person with a twinkle in his eye, it would, indeed, be a fitting tribute.

We dedicated the reunion to the memory of Mr. Grey, and many attendees learned of his passing only upon arriving at the event.

The school of which he was principal now bears his name, and a memorial plaque mounted on the wall not far from the spot in which he posed for his final portrait remembers him as "a caring and committed educator." Although I cannot argue with any of the traits officially attributed to him, there is no mention of the quick temper and surly disposition for which students may actually most remember him.

With the passing of years, however, these characteristics have become more endearing. Time has softened the rough edges of what now appears to have been harmless bluster. Still, it gives me deep satisfaction to know that for a few unlikely minutes, he let his guard down long enough for me to glimpse another side of the  man behind the scowl. It is the way in which I will forever remember Mr. Grey.

And I have the pictures to prove it.

Cowboys on Bicycles

One of the things I learned when I was a cowboy is that you need a heck of a lot of stuff. First, you need a horse. This is, perhaps, the most essential item, as cowboys who do not have horses are actually not cowboys at all. These are the individuals who, by default, became the general store-keepers, telegraph operators, and saloon proprietors in the towns where the cowboys periodically stopped to have a drink and smash a few chairs in the bar. These horseless men did not even look like cowboys. Even if they had owned a horse, it would be the type that did not know how to gallop, and could do little more than slowly pull a small wagon into town and back. Anyway, they were not rugged-looking enough to be cowboys. Some of these non-cowboys wore spectacles and a good many of them were also bald, a feature that precluded gainful employment in the cowboy industry.

Another thing you need to be a cowboy is a good supply of cows. Hence, the name — cowboys. These always seemed to be plentiful out on the dusty plains, and most were either wild or had broken free from their enclosures and were in need of roping and branding. Then you need a cowboy hat, cowboy boots, chaps, rope, saddlebags, and, of course, a gun. The list of mandatory gear and accessories goes on and on. The gun is also of extreme importance and finds nearly constant use in the presence of bad guys who were sufficiently numerous in the old west. Cowboys, in fact, spend more time shooting at bad guys than chasing after their namesake, the cows.

Everything I know about being a cowboy, I learned from watching TV in the 1950s. If you paid close attention, it was like going to cowboy school. By paying attention, I learned to always count the number of bullets fired at you so you could tell when the bad guy's six-shooter had been depleted of ammunition. Another thing I noticed by paying close attention was that the best cowboys all have one very important thing—a theme song, or what I called galloping music. *Dun-ta-da-dun, Ta-da-dun*. It wasn't something a cowboy had to think about though, and many seemed not even to be aware of the music that came out of nowhere whenever a cowboy mounted his horse and began riding somewhere in a hurry.

Having none of the requisite essentials to actually be a cowboy, I learned that all of this can be overcome with one thing: a good imagination. My first horse was a fifty-five-gallon metal drum that was horizontally mounted on an X-shaped frame near the back door of my childhood home in Boston. I believe it may originally have contained oil of some sort, but when I banged my pretend spurs into its sides, it sounded quite empty. It was just the right size and height to qualify as a horse. Not like one of those little toy horse heads you pull around on the end of a stick. For one thing, there was nothing to sit on with one of those things. You were pretty much just running around with a stick between your legs. Not at all like what I imagined being on a real horse might feel like.

My metal drum was sufficiently high enough off the ground that I had to stand on a wooden crate to mount it. And once atop the barrel, I had to spread my legs so wide to straddle it that it was easy to imagine a real horse beneath me. The only drawback to a barrel was that it did not actually go anywhere. After five minutes of hard riding at a full gallop, when I dismounted, I was still right beside the back door. If my cowboy services were needed in the front yard, I had to run around on foot past the fire escape with guns drawn, and then squeeze through a gap in the fence. I pretended that my horse simply would not have fit through the narrow opening, and that I had left him behind and out of sight to facilitate a quick getaway should the need arise. This is where a good imagination really came in handy.

Growing up in the fifties, it was not difficult to get caught up in the appeal of the whole cowboy thing. It was hard to avoid it. Almost every other TV show was a western. *Roy Rogers, Hopalong Cassidy, Wild Bill Hickock, Gunsmoke, Wagon Train, The Lone Ranger, Wyatt Earp, Rawhide, Maverick, The Cisco Kid.* You couldn't get away from them. I didn't realize it at the time, but my heroes were unrealistic and glorified caricatures living in a sterilized, fantasy version of the western frontier. This also took a lot of imagination. Or at least blind acceptance. For the most part, the ones who were not actually employed as lawmen simply drifted from town to town cleansing the old west of villains before riding off into the sunset. Many of my heroes were actually homeless vagrants with no visible means of support. They slept outdoors under the stars, yet their clothing was always freshly laundered and pressed. Everything they owned fit into a slim leather saddlebag. They did not appear to carry those small incidental items so essential for living even in the world of a hundred years ago. Whenever they stopped for the night and built a campfire, they always managed to materialize plenty of food as well as a large coffee pot and tin mugs from which to drink. Yet you never saw their horses piled high with kitchen utensils and groceries. This would have seriously hampered their ability to mount their horse in one acrobatic leap from behind.

Nor did they burden themselves with wallets or toothbrushes. The thought of Hopalong Cassidy brushing his teeth would have destroyed the mystique. Neither could we imagine the Lone Ranger removing his mask to shave and wash his face, although he was always clean-shaven with highly polished cheeks. It wasn't realism. It was a romanticized lifestyle that every eight-year-old boy lived vicariously through his favorite cowboy star.

Everything in my life during the 1950s was centered around cowboys. My favorite breakfast cereal was Kellogg's

Sugar Corn Pops. Not because I particularly liked the taste, but because their TV commercials featured Wild Bill Hickock's sidekick, Jingles, who, with guns blazing, informed us that they were "shot with sugar, through and through." I ate the puffy, yellowish nuggets with my Hopalong Cassidy spoon and washed them down with cocoa from my Ranger Joe mug. All I ever wanted for my birthday was more cowboy accessories. Cowboy lunchboxes, cowboy clothing, cowboy books, pencil boxes, games, pajamas, bedroom lamps. Even my birthday cake featured cowboy decorations in the form of tiny, plastic men attempting to lasso a bucking bronco, while at the same time having their feet firmly planted in green frosting.

Living much of my childhood as a cowboy in Massachusetts might have made me self-conscious had it not been for the fact that every other kid I knew was also a cowboy. The Sears catalog was full of cowboy stuff, and walking into a toy store you could find anything you wanted. As long as what you wanted was cowboy stuff. The part of my cowboy outfit of which I was most proud was a real suede jacket. Unlike many other articles of children's western apparel, it did not have the name of a popular cowboy embroidered in script lettering to resemble lariat rope, or anything so garish. What it did have was the softest, saddle-brown leather and a yoke of contrasting lighter tan. But the coupe de grace—the icing on the cake—was fringe. Fringe across the bottom of the yoke on both the front and the back. Fringe trailing the full length of each sleeve. And fringe hanging at the waist that went all the way around the entire jacket. No matter which direction I was facing, envious people could see my fringe as it gently reacted to even my most subtle gestures. Not stiff like some cheaper cowboy clothing.

Even after I accidentally spilled Coca-Cola on the sleeve, the fringe remained supple and flexible. I was hyperconscious of my fringe and took every possible opportunity to make sure its many admirers were impressed with the way it responded to the slightest movement. I lingered momentarily whenever I reached for the car door handle, and I got into the habit of pointing a lot. Anything that required my arm to be extended caused the fringe to dance and sway, which brought me great pleasure. For this reason I always kept knocking at my friend's door long after I heard his footsteps approaching from inside the house. It was this behavior that caused Tommy McPhee to comment not on the fact that I was particularly well-dressed, but on the possibility that I might be going deaf.

Ambling into a grocery store dressed in full cowboy apparel, or walking through the center of town with a six-shooter holstered at each hip seemed quite normal in the 1950s. The only occasion at which I was not permitted to wear any cowboy gear was Sunday school. It gave me great pleasure, however, to know that beneath my respectable little shirt and bow tie, I sat quietly in my Roy Rogers underwear.

But dressing the part was just the beginning. One had

to play the part to get the full effect. Playing cowboys was when we actually got to immerse ourselves in the cowboy lifestyle. By emulating the TV cowboys, it was easy to see yourself climbing not onto a bicycle, but mounting a horse. Cars were stagecoaches, the hill out back, a cliff, and the slight depression below it, a canyon. The shed out back became a bunkhouse, except when it was needed for a jail. My first two-wheeler was small, but adequately served my need to gallop around the neighborhood creating rising clouds of dust by skidding to a gravelly stop as I sang my theme music. *Dun-ta-da-dun. Ta-da-dun.* I never used my kickstand, but instead, let the bike fall, dismounting in one effortless motion, knowing that my horse would stay unattended without straying, and come whenever I whistled just like on TV. The handlebars were reins, the seat, a saddle, and the pedals, stirrups. All it took was a little imagination.

Acting out cowboy mini-dramas was my single most fulfilling pastime. Improvisational brawls, shootouts, chase scenes, all came remarkably alive as my friends and I imitated the actions of the cowboys on TV. We each played our action-packed roles with great enthusiasm, becoming our favorite western heroes and insisting that the others call us by our proper names. This led to inevitable discussions of hero hierarchy and arguments about which TV cowboy had the right to beat up the other. Mostly though, we just teamed up and went after the bad guys. In my neighborhood there was never a shortage of kids who wanted to play the part of the outlaws. Chase scenes would typically end in a flourish of simulated fisticuffs which, for the outlaws, always turned out badly. If they were lucky, it meant they'd get a chance to get shot in the gut and fall to the ground, dying an agonizing death that sometimes lasted for minutes. The good thing about playing an outlaw was that when you were finished dying, you could come back to life as another outlaw. Those were the rules.

The one role that no kid in the neighborhood wanted to play was the sidekick. This was something that virtually every cowboy hero on TV had. In the scheme of relative importance, it wasn't as necessary as, say, a horse, but it was right up there. They all had one. The Lone Ranger had Tonto, The Cisco Kid had Pancho, Gene Autry had Pat Buttram. Playing the sidekick, however, did not hold the glamour and the prestige of being the hero. There were few redeeming roles to act out when playing the sidekick. You didn't even get to die. Ironically, there was no shortage of kids who wanted to play outlaws and take a fall in the name of justice, yet when it came time to choose who would be the sidekicks, the role actually ranked below that of a dead guy. So for the most part, the roles of sidekicks were relegated to the younger kids who were still able to be bullied.

It was easy to tell the good cowboys from the bad guys. Again, we took our cues from TV westerns. In an apparent unspoken rule of thumb, the printed bandanna that was worn by all cowboys held the key. The bandanna was folded into a triangle and knotted around the neck, leaving two pointed ends to stick out like little rabbit ears. Here's where the good guy/bad guy code of the old west comes into play. The good guys wore their bandannas knotted in the front so that the triangle hung at the back of the neck. The bad guys, on the other hand, as a considerate gesture to facilitate easy identification as fair targets, turned their bandannas and wore them with the triangle in front.

This not only accommodated the whims of fashion, but also provided the bad guys with a convenient flap of cloth with which to cover their faces when it came time to rob a stagecoach. Advance planning of such an endeavor would have allowed adequate time to both turn the bandanna around *and* pull up the flap, but, apparently, bandits were prone to spur-of-the-moment criminal activity, necessitating the need to cover one's face at a moment's notice.

When I wasn't outside playing cowboys, I was in my bedroom playing cowboys. In my room I kept dozens of little plastic cowboys so that I could act out complicated cowboy scenarios in miniature. The tiny plastic pieces were molded from single, vivid colors of soft plastic. If a tiny cowboy wore a bright green shirt, that meant he also had a bright green face, bright green hair, and a bright green pistol. Most of the cowboys were formed into a perpetually bow-legged stance that allowed them to ride their little, plastic horses in a most convincing manner, though allowing them to stand only flatfooted and awkwardly, not unlike the actual actors in the TV westerns. Other plastic cowboys were molded into various useful poses. One vivid yellow cowboy stood swinging a yellow lariat. Two more cowboys, one blue and one white, held pistols in their outstretched hands waiting to be shown what or whom to aim at. One cowboy was intended to sit on the seat of a wagon or stage coach, but because there were no reins for him to hold, the way in which he leaned forward with his arms on his knees made it look as if he were sitting on the toilet. But that required a great deal of imagination.

I was also able to project myself into the cowboy fantasy by drawing pictures of cowboy scenes. Most involved cowboys riding on deformed horses and shooting at each other. Careful study of each drawing would reveal an entire adventure story captured in the meticulous detail. By following the trajectory of each bullet you could tell who was shooting at whom. And you could tell the bad guys, of course, by the way they wore their bandannas. In all of my

pictures, I always envisioned myself as the hero I was drawing, though I never included my eyeglasses. They would have made me look too much like the general storekeeper.

My fascination with cowboys lasted as long as their popularity on television. But it didn't go easily. I was well into grade school before I thought of my bike as having wheels and not legs. And to this day, my family still calls chocolate chip cookies "cowboy cookies." When you've been a cowboy for as long as I was — once you've tasted prairie dust, and shot as many outlaws as I have, it's not so easy to just let it all go and sing in the youth choir or join the cub scouts. I threw myself into the role and took it seriously. It was how I lived my cowboy childhood. It's how I do everything. Enthusiastically. Unabashedly. And slightly out of touch with reality.

A Promising Childhood

It was during one of those whiny episodes when Mom was making me come in from playing in the yard to take a bath and get ready for bed. It was a Friday night in early summer and it sure didn't feel like eight o'clock. It wasn't even getting dark yet. It was at that moment that I made a promise to myself. When I became an adult, I would stay up all night, never take a bath, and play all the time. Oh, and I would eat candy bars for dinner. The latter was an after-thought thrown into the promisory mix while I was on a roll.

"Billy's mother lets him stay out," I sobbed, kicking the dirt and walking toward the back door slowly enough to allow for a last minute change of parental heart. Grown-ups just don't understand kids.

Then with the impeccable timing that could only have come as the result of a preplanned, coordinated effort, Billy's mother leaned out of their front door and yelled, "Billy! Time to come in."

"See what I mean? It's not fair." I looked to Billy for support, but he was already halfway home, running at top speed. It made me wonder if Billy's mom gave him some kind of special reward for showing up on command. Could it be that bath night at Billy's house was accompanied by ice cream?

Billy had barely reached the far side of the street when his mother reissued her demand with slightly more volume and considerably more agitation. "Billy!" It was definitely not an ice cream voice. It sounded as if Billy would have more to deal with when he got home than merely washing behind his ears. Maybe he had once again left the cage door of his pet lizard open as he was prone to do. Or perhaps he had discovered an entirely new way of testing the parental resolve of his beleaguered mother.

Billy was good at being bad. He once dragged the garden hose in through a downstairs window to make a vat of mud in his kitchen sink, but had become distracted and had forgotten to turn off the water. I didn't get to see the final result of his efforts, but the entire neighborhood could hear his mother commenting on it. Mud can be a lot of fun, but I've found it's usually better to keep it outside.

At any rate, it was clear that I was going to have to fight this battle by myself. I was tired of always being told what to do. Adult authority and its arbitrary rules was all that stood between me and the total freedom to do whatever I wanted. But waiting until I was an adult seemed an unacceptably long duration. The amount of time it would take to achieve such status was unimaginable. No one could wait that long. It seemed inconceivable to me that grown-ups had at one time been children themselves. Somehow, it was easier to think of them springing into the world as fully formed, little adults, perhaps just a bit smaller, and without the neckties and lipstick.

Now that summer had arrived, I had seen my bedtime extended by half an hour, but still saw no reason for a bedtime in the first place.

"If you stay up too late," came the official motherly response to my grievance, "you'll be cranky."

"No I won't!" I sulked, heaving my shoulders down for dramatic effect.

"See? You're getting cranky already."

"No, I'm cranky because you won't *let* me stay up late." I loved it when I could turn her own reasoning around, forcing her to see the logic of my wisdom. I started to complain that if I went to bed this early, I'd just be lying awake in my room, but I had previously had occasion to use that argument to no avail. Sometimes you just can't reason with adults.

By the time I had finished marinating in my tepid bath water, and had watched the last of its dingy residue gurgle down the drain, I was actually getting kind of sleepy. But I couldn't let Mom know that. She had come in to give me a bath towel while she picked up my dirty clothes from the floor where I had dropped them. As I was drying off, I couldn't keep my head from tipping back and letting out this huge yawn. "I'm not tired," I immediately insisted. "Taking a bath always makes me yawn." I felt compelled to casually mention this, though, somehow, saying it out loud sounded even more defensive than I had imagined it might. Mom didn't say anything, but grinned at me and lifted one eyebrow. I was glad she didn't say anything or make a big deal of it because I was also starting to get a little cranky. Billy's mom would have raised her voice and turned it into a big lecture. I could almost hear her yelling, "I knew you were tired. Didn't I tell you you were tired? Listen to me when I tell you you're tired." I'm glad my mom doesn't yell at me. Then again, I never made our kitchen look like the beach at low tide.

When I awoke the next morning, all traces of crankiness had been erased by a good night's sleep. More parental mandates, however, were about to be issued. There was the obligatory task of picking up my room, a wholly unnecessary activity in my opinion. Never once in my entire six years had I ever heard either of my parents say that they were going upstairs to pick up their room.

"No one's gonna see my room. I don't care if it's messy," I complained from behind a scattering of toys as, one by one, I shuttled them to more suitable locations. Admittedly, putting them away seemed only a minor inconvenience. Still, I would rather have been outside playing. Billy was outside. I could hear him throwing rocks at our neighbor's fence. "When I grow up," I ranted, mumbling another promise to myself, "I'm not gonna put anything away. I *like* the way it looks. I like being able to see everything. Grownups just don't understand kids."

Upon completing the tedious chore of compacting all of my belongings into a tiny closet by forcing the closet door against the compressed mound of toys, I made my way downstairs with the specific intention of heading outside. My mother, who was busy playing in some soapy water with a bunch of dishes, intercepted me without looking up.

"Are all your toys picked up?"

"Yes." I answered. "Can I go outside and play?"

"You didn't just throw them in your closet, did you?"

"No," I lied. It really wasn't a lie. I didn't actually *throw* them.

Mom said I could finally go outside, and then she went back to playing in the soapy water. "No one tells grown-ups what to do," I grumbled as I headed out the back door. "They get to do whatever they want. Mostly fun stuff."

Out in the backyard, my father was lugging trash to the car for a trip to the dump. That sounded like fun, too, and I asked him if I could go along.

"Did you pick up your room?"

"Yes." I rolled my eyes as if he should have known that I'd just had this conversation. I climbed up onto the wide bench seat on the passenger side of the car as Dad finished piling trash and other debris into the back. Grown-ups get to do fun things like go to the dump all the time, I thought to myself. I love the dump. Grinning with anticipation, I made another mental promise to myself that when I grow up, I would go to the dump as often as possible.

After about a ten minute drive, we pulled into the landfill site on Route 2. Saturday being the busiest day, we had to wait while other dads ahead of us unloaded their trash. Finally a slot opened up and we backed in between two other cars right to the edge of the drop-off so that the back of our car was almost overhanging the cavernous pit that gaped beneath us. I usually spent the final ten feet or so of our approach pleading with Dad in a high-pitched, panicky voice, "Okay, that's close enough. Whoa! Please! You can stop now!" That was the only part of going to the dump that was not fun, but Dad seemed to enjoy seeing how close he could get to the edge without having the rear tires actually go over the embankment.

The dump was enormously entertaining. Huge mountains of refuse rose from the floor of the canyon like oceans of colorful salad. Jagged pieces of nondescript metal poked up from heaps of cardboard and glass. Sometimes part of a baby carriage or bicycle extended a twisted appendage up through the jumble like a drowning swimmer. But mostly, you couldn't tell what things were unless you started digging through the rubble and lifting pieces to see what was under them. Dad descended into the pit to do this all the time. He had to wade through piles of trash, but we sometimes came home with interesting junk that other people had disposed of. Sometimes, we'd bring home almost as much as we brought to throw away. Dad had once brought home a huge Atwater-Kent radio that didn't work. It was the kind that was full of those heavy glass tubes that glow when you turn it on. It sat down in our cellar for years until Mom finally made him take it back to the dump. Dad didn't let me dig through the trash because of all the sharp edges, but he did let me throw glass bottles into the pit to see if I could break them on something. There were also numerous fires burning across the vast landscape of refuse, and it was fun to see if you could throw something into the flames causing them to retaliate with a flurry of sparks.

The dump, I thought, was as much fun as an amusement park. Maybe more, because you couldn't throw bottles at an amusement park. But you couldn't go to the dump if you were just a kid. You had to be an adult, or at least with an adult. Once again, I mused, grown-ups got to do fun stuff whenever they wanted. I'm going to love being an adult when no one tells me what to do, and I can do whatever I want.

The last of the bottles having been hurled into the abyss, and Dad content that he had salvaged as much as he could for the day, we both took our seats in the car a little grubbier than when we got out. As we pulled out of our parking slot on the edge of the drop-off, I saw another dad excitedly dredging something up from the bottomless piles of debris. It looked like an Atwater-Kent radio.

By the time we got home, Mom had finished playing in the sink, and was making peanut butter and jelly sandwiches for lunch. She let me help her once, and it was a lot of fun, but I made a pretty big mess, so now I just let her have all the fun of making lunch. Before I could eat though, she made me go wash my hands even though I'd just had a bath last night. Sometimes I think grown-ups just like telling kids what to do.

After lunch, Dad went down cellar to play with a hammer and some nails, and Mom said she was going to buy groceries. Mom said I could help with either if I wanted. They both sounded like fun, but I chose grocery shopping because it meant I would get to push the grocery cart and there was an outside chance that I might get to pick out a box of cereal.

The criteria for selecting cereal had little to do with whether or not I actually liked the taste, and had everything to do with the prize that came free inside the box. After careful deliberation I chose a box of Sugar Frosted Flakes because of a compelling depiction of a Navy frogman on the front of the box. He was shown ascending from the depths of shark-infested water as he kicked his huge frogman flippers in a flurry of bubbles. Free inside was a lifelike replica of him that, according to the words on the box, would actually dive and resurface when placed in water. It was tough deciding between that and another box that came with a free bird whistle inside, but in the end, the vivid frogman illustration and the promise of "endless hours of fun" won me over.

Had I been an adult, there were a lot of things at the grocery store that I would have bought. Mom walked right past most of them and, instead, filled our carriage with things like toilet paper, laundry detergent, and canned peas. She let me add a jar of Bosco to our cart, but said "no" to a fun-looking box of cookies in the shape of animals.

The first thing I did when we got home was to tear into the Frosted Flakes. I jammed my hand down into the box and rummaged around until I found the frogman lying at the very bottom, sealed inside a cellophane package. He was made of blue plastic, and was about the length of my little finger. He was standing on a capsule that looked like a tiny, upside-down thimble which I discovered was the secret to his diving and resurfacing ability. On the bottom of the tiny thimble was a metal cap about the size of an aspirin tablet, and after prying it off with my fingernail, I filled the capsule with a small amount of baking soda according to the directions. After replacing the metal cap, I dropped the frogman into water and watched him quickly sink to the bottom. After several seconds, an air bubble formed at a small pinhole in the metal cap. It was tiny, but created enough buoyancy to lift the frogman back up to the surface where he turned on his side and released the bubble like a tiny fart. He then returned to the bottom to begin the process again.

This cycle repeated a number of times until the baking soda had been depleted. This happened at precisely the same time that I lost interest in the procedure. The picture on the cereal box was far more exciting than what was inside it, and watching a piece of blue plastic go up and down in the bathroom sink held much less fascination than did the picture of the man returning from the murky depths of the ocean bottom. The highly anticipated endless hours of fun had turned out to be a few minutes of disappointing boredom. I should have gone for the bird whistle. When I'm an adult, I promised myself, I'll get them both.

I'd been back downstairs drawing pictures for quite some time when Mom and Dad informed me that I should go pee because we were going for a ride.

"Where?" I asked.

"Oh, just for a ride," came my dad's reply.

Every once in a while we'd just get into the car and drive without knowing where we'd end up. It was another fun thing that adults did, and as long as I got to go along, it was one of the times I didn't mind being told what to do. Sometimes we'd find ourselves on a back road having no idea where we were.

"Are we lost?" I wouldn't have minded if the answer had been "yes," but Dad's answer was always, "not exactly."

Sometimes we'd be driving along being not exactly lost and all of a sudden we'd come out at a place that looked familiar. Both Mom and Dad would smile and say something like, "Oh, I know where we are." It was like a game that adults got to play that always had a happy surprise ending. Being an adult will be a lot of fun. I promised myself that I would play this game all the time between trips to the dump.

Sometimes on one of our drives we'd actually go someplace. Once we went to an airport and watched airplanes take off and land. Another time we drove to the top of a huge hill and had a picnic. You could see mountains in the distance and there were cows in a field right in front of us. Today we'd end up two towns away from home at a place called Kimball's Farm, though I got the feeling that it was a decision made only when we found ourselves nearby. Kimball's had cows too, but the best thing they had was ice cream. The parking lot was usually nearly full, and even though there were several windows at which to order, enormous crowds of people waited in long lines at each. We joined the shortest one and watched a steady stream of people pass by precariously balancing huge mountains of ice cream with whipped cream on top. My parents always ordered something called a Kimball's Special. It consisted of three giant scoops of different flavors of ice cream with three different sauces, tons of whipped cream, and three cherries. It was like getting three sundaes lined up in one huge cardboard tray.

Being that it was nearing dinner time and we had not yet eaten, against my better judgement I blurted out, "Won't we spoil our dinner?" to which my mother answered, "This *is* our dinner."

My joy could barely be contained as my eyes widened and my mouth stretched to the absolute limits of its smile capacity. I could not have imagined a more rapturous end to the day. The only thing better than being allowed to order anything I wanted at Kimball's was not having to needlessly fill up on dinner first. Going straight to dessert—now that was my idea of what being an adult was all about. All of the fun and none of the rules. It was at that precise moment that I decided to reconsider a promise I had made to myself. Something about always eating candy bars for dinner. Right there as I stood in line anticipating my three-course dinner consisting of a pile of ice cream as big as my head, I revised my earlier promise. I would not always eat candy bars for dinner. Sometimes I'd go to Kimball's.

Rest in Peace

It was deathly quiet. So absolute was the silence that, at times, the enormity of it seemed capable of swallowing my very existence. I lay motionless in the dark wondering if I would ever be able to fall back asleep, and strained with heightened intensity to perceive even the faintest sound. My ears bristled with the awareness that there was nothing whatsoever to be heard. The only assurance that I had not gone totally and inexplicably deaf came from the muffled pumping of my own heart and the slight rustling of my clothing when I occasionally attempted to adjust my position.

There was not the slightest distant hint that another living being existed within a thousand miles. Yet, at the same time, I was acutely aware that scattered around me in close proximity were the horizontal corpses of hundreds of former citizens of the small town where I grew up.

Boxborough, Massachusetts, was a sleepy, little community some thirty or so miles west of Boston, although it might as well have been in another time zone. During the 1960s when I lived there, fewer than seven hundred individuals called this place home—not enough even for our own post office. (In Massachusetts, a town needed at least a thousand residents before it was endowed with such conveniences of modern civilization.) Many of the roads in town had only recently seen pavement, and the town's only school accommodated grades one through six only.

The Blanchard School was so tiny, in fact, that as a sixth grader, I was placed in the same classroom with the same teacher as my sister who was a grade behind me. Mr. Lahar was adept at juggling the lessons, although it was impossible not to eavesdrop on what the other grade was learning. My sister got a preview. I got a refresher course.

The whole of grade six for the entire town numbered fifteen. My sister's class, grade five, only nine. Not only did the entirety of both grades for all of Boxborough sit in one room with one teacher, but the school's small size also compelled him to take on the role of principal as well. In a small town, not all public needs are adequately fulfilled.

Even the smallest towns, however, have always managed to set aside a certain amount of public land for use as a burial ground. It was often, in fact, the first matter of business to which early inhabitants attended as they pushed their way into a largely unexplored continent. It was on a dark country road that Boxborough's small cemetery quietly sprawled behind ancient stone walls. And it was here that I would spend the night, along with my good friend, Bruce Prowten, in a cramped and dark crypt trying to sleep as if the situation was a normal occurrence in our adolescent lives.

It was mid-December of my fourteenth year. I lay huddled in a sleeping bag on the dirt floor of the single underground cemetery vault that rose under a mound of earth in the middle of the graveyard. The darkness enveloped me, if you'll forgive the expression, like a tomb. Outside, a thin blanket of snow smothered the faint remnants of whatever sound might otherwise have reached me, though, in this part of town, even during the day, there was barely a passing car to breach the silence.

In all respects, the town was a pretty quiet place. Not much happened in Boxborough, and although it was the lifestyle they themselves had chosen, townspeople had to drive to Acton, the neighboring town, if they wanted any kind of stimulus at all.

There was no crime in Boxborough. It had no police department, although it did have a part-time constable, George Robinson, who was also the school janitor, the dog catcher, school bus driver, and fence viewer. (I never did learn exactly what duties he was expected to perform in the latter capacity.) I had telephoned him earlier that day for the specific intent of informing him that should anyone report seeing lights emanating from the burial ground in the middle of the night, that this should not be taken as a cause for concern. In all likelihood, it would just be me getting up for a midnight snack.

Less than a mile north of the cemetery was Boxborough's town center. The center of town was barely that, and could be considered so only by an extreme stretch of one's imagination. It was so designated not by virtue of anything remotely resembling a town center. Its one outstanding feature was the fact that two roads crossed each other, giving rise to the need for one of the town's few stop signs. The clever naming of one of the streets as Middle Road provided, perhaps, the only hint of the location's significance. There was no shopping district. No sidewalk. No traffic light. Not a single amenity that would cause an outsider to consider for one moment that this, indeed, was the center of anything.

A modest, wooden church sat unassumingly back from the road on one corner. Diagonally across and set on a slight rise was Pop Moore's variety store. It was the only store of any kind in the entire town, and the variety left much to be desired. Pop was already elderly when I moved into town with my parents, and how anyone could make a living at such an endeavor was beyond me. Ancient candy in yellowing wrappers was visible under a generous coating of dust, and I'm quite certain that companies had not yet begun to print expiration dates on packaging, or much of what he sold would have been deemed unfit for human consumption.

Mostly, it was just us kids that made up his customer base. I cannot remember ever seeing a single adult in Pop Moore's store except to buy a Sunday paper, although there must have been the occasional brave soul that wandered in for a package of fossilized hot dogs, or a can of tuna left over from World War II.

When Pop died in the 1960s, his store died with him. No one was brave enough (or foolish enough) to continue his legacy by trying to capture the business of passing motorists that on busy days must have numbered at least in the dozens.

The only other business of any kind in town was a single Gulf service station a quarter mile further along Route 111. I say service, and not gas station, because Fred Joyce would come out to greet everyone who stopped as he pumped gas with a smile, washed your windshield, and offered to check the oil and fluid levels of all sorts. I think he might have just been glad to talk to someone, but regardless, we were always happy to stop and give him the three dollars it took to fill our gas tank.

It was barely a ten minute walk from this bustling metropolis to where the gentle folks of Boxborough had, since the mid-1700s, deposited their dead. Long rows of carved headstones were tilted at odd angles in uneven rows. Ruts worn into the earth by wagon wheels and, later, automobiles, provided the means to navigate its length in two directions, but mostly, one had to walk over wide, grassy patches to access a particular section.

The vault in which I now lay was inconspicuous from the outside, despite its prominent location in the middle of the cemetery. From the back, it was nothing more than a grassy mound rising to a height of perhaps eight feet from otherwise flat terrain. The front of the vault, the side facing the two ruts that passed nearby, featured some modest stonework of large granite slabs into one of which was carved the date, "1901." A heavy iron door swung outward, as the cramped interior was not sufficiently spacious to allow for an inward trajectory. The doorway was barely as tall as myself, as I distinctly recall having to duck to gain access to the cramped quarters inside.

It was now the middle of the night. The temperature had dropped precipitously throughout the evening, and even inside the vault, I could now feel that my hands were

getting cold even through my winter gloves. After what seemed like an eternity of deafening silence, I decided to break one arm free from my down-filled cocoon and reach for my flashlight. It flicked on with the loudest sound I had heard in hours. Folding back the cuff of my winter coat, I was surprised, if not a little disappointed, to discover that it was not yet 11:00 p.m. I was certain that the first welcome rays of dawn would soon be upon me, but I now realized that

I had slept for perhaps only an hour.

I lifted my head from the cold floor to follow the beam of light that extended out from my right hand. The yellowish glow projected creepy shadows onto the inside of the tomb that tonight served as my sleeping chamber. I turned to my left where my roommate, Bruce, huddled under a large mound of sleeping bag facing the opposite wall. Except for the ski hat partially protruding at the top end, he looked eerily like a wrapped cadaver. It made me once again aware that we were closely surrounded by hundreds of dead bodies. My overactive imagination recalled a story recounted by a schoolmate in which a body that had been buried prematurely had scratched its way to the surface and gone on a killing spree in revenge. He swore the event was documented by reliable sources.

"You asleep?" I whispered.

"Nope," came Bruce's weak reply through a sleeping bag and three layers of sweaters and a wool coat.

I slowly moved the light back and forth over the inside of the chamber. A brick ceiling arched over us at a height that made standing upright impossible except in the very center of the vault. The entire chamber was only about eight feet wide and, perhaps, ten feet in length. At one end, we had left the single iron door slightly ajar on its massive rusted hinges to provide an exchange of oxygen during the night, as the air inside was dead and musty and hung like it had not moved in years. With each breath, we inhaled the pungent odor of dead leaves that lay scattered over the floor, blown in over what I imagined to have been decades.

"You hungry?" asked Bruce in a voice hushed enough so as not to arouse any patrons resting in our immediate vicinity.

"Nah," I breathed back. Actually, I could have done with a Snickers bar or some other form of sustenance, but the thought of taking off my gloves and rummaging through my knapsack in the dark seemed like more trouble than it was worth. The resulting sounds produced by the foraging would also have provided a convenient cover for any deranged prowler attempting to sneak up on us and butcher us with a large axe. I had also brought a canteen of ginger ale, but in the frigid air, that seemed much less appealing than it had some hours earlier when I searched my parents' refrigerator looking for provisions.

Now, entombed in a cramped graveyard vault, with hours still before we would see daylight, we lay awake, hyper-alert, as we studied the masonry walls that seemed to close in on us more with each passing minute. We lied with our feet toward the door, our heads at the opposite end of the chamber, which provided a good view of the intruder that we were sure would appear at any moment. I could see the newspaper headlines already: *"Frightened Farmer Slays Slumbering Teens He Fears Are Corpses Rising from Tomb."*

Through the narrow door opening we could see that more snow was now beginning to fall. I directed the flashlight beam out into the endless black where small, icy flakes landed with audible clicks like the ticking of a clock. There was an eerie sense of timelessness as each measured breath marked a mere few seconds of a night that stretched out endlessly before us. I thought I had heard the barking of a hopelessly distant dog, and I held my breath hoping to confirm the fact that the sound was, indeed, miles away. I strained to hear, but the sound did not repeat.

An instant later, my blood ran cold and my heart almost stopped beating. Outside, from on top of the vault, a pile of snow came crashing down in front of the doorway as if it had been thrown there by someone—or some*thing*. My eyes widened and adrenaline pumped knowing that there was but one way out of the crypt, and that was directly into the throes of whatever was out there waiting for us.

Before I had time to consider all of the unspeakable possibilities, a man bundled up in winter clothing jumped from on top of the vault and landed outside with his back to us just feet from the bottoms of our sleeping bags. As he turned to face our cowering forms, I pointed my flashlight directly into his eyes hoping that the resulting temporarily blindness it would cause would give us time to scramble past him and run screaming for our lives into the snowy blackness. Of course, we were buried in half a dozen layers of long underwear, sweaters, coats, ski hats, and scarves with sleeping bags wrapped around us for good measure, so we weren't going anywhere.

And then the strangest thing happened. In a moment that was at once terrifying and comforting, I recognized the face of the man standing before us as that of my father who had casually dropped in to assess our accommodations.

"How are you boys doin'?" he asked as if he were popping his head into the living room where we had just been watching television. "The weather forecast is for about a foot of heavy snow. I just wanted to make sure you still wanted to stay."

"Yeah, we're fine," we said, glancing sideways toward each other as if to silently add, "Aren't we?"

After declining half a Snickers bar and a swig of ginger ale, he ducked back out into the cold and disappeared along with our last chance for a warm, comfortable ride home.

Soon afterward, I decided to forsake the cold and get up to have one final and lasting pee. Not wanting particularly to venture out into the open graveyard, I decided to stoop just inside the vault door and aim a perfect trajectory through the narrow opening, being cautiously alert, of course, in case the axe-wielding marauder was still prowling about, and lest I return missing a vital part of my anatomy.

After a night of fidgety sleep, punctuated by frequent references to my wristwatch, we at long last awoke to the first weak rays of daylight to discover that about ten inches of wet snow had accumulated in front of the vault door. Because the door opened outward, it took all of our strength with Bruce and me pushing against it to create an opening that was finally large enough to squeeze through with all of our belongings. I also noticed that the bologna sandwich that I had brought for breakfast as well as the remainder of my ginger ale were both frozen solid.

Trudging through the fresh snow on our way out of the cemetery, everything seemed friendlier and less threatening than it had only hours before. Quite peaceful, really. Reading the inscriptions on the rows of headstones as we tramped our way toward Stow Road, it was clear that most inhabitants had died hundreds of years earlier, and if they had been inclined to break free of their entombment and go prowling about looking to avenge their untimely burial, it is likely they would have done so before now. What a difference a little daylight and a partial night's sleep makes.

It was not the first, nor was it to be the last time Bruce and I would endeavor to satisfy our oddly unique obsession of sleeping with the dead. We did, however, decide that waiting for more favorable weather conditions might be to our great advantage.

One such fellow we seemed to favor for such sleepovers was Nathan Whitney. Mr. Whitney was to us a very special individual, perhaps because my friends and I were among the very few privileged to know his whereabouts. You see, despite his having been deceased for a very long time, Mr. Whitney did not reside in a cemetery.

The only way, in fact, one would locate his modest grave site was if you already knew where it was. The grandfather of one of my friends had learned of it's location from his own father when he was a boy. Apparently, the secret whereabouts of Mr. Whitney had been handed down for generations like an heirloom pocket watch, and we were quite certain that no written record of its location existed. We thought it probable, in fact, that there was no public record of its very existence.

The secret coordinates lay just off Burroughs Road, a narrow country road that curved its way through miles of swamp and dense woods passing barely a house on its way. It was at an otherwise nondescript bend in the road that by climbing the stone wall on the south side and heading off through the dense woods at a certain angle, one would eventually arrive at the final resting place of Nathan Whitney.

The site was marked by a thin, but finely-carved slate headstone in remarkably good condition. It was so well camouflaged among the dense woods, however, that you could stand a mere ten feet from the dark gray marker and not see it. The stone, barely two feet in height, featured a carved depiction of a distinguished-looking gentleman in a powdered wig, just beneath which, in fancy lettering still exceptionally crisp in its detail, read, "Here lies ye body of Mr. Nathan Whitney. Died with ye small pox Apriel ye 11, AD 1761 in ye 69 year of his age."

This, of course, explained the other characteristics that made the site so extraordinary. First of all, we loved thinking about the fact that he had lived his entire life before the United States was even a country. We found it exceedingly fascinating to imagine what the surrounding countryside and villages were like at such a formative time in our country's history.

Then, of course, there was the whole smallpox thing. I mean, wow. *Smallpox!* And here he was lying only a few feet below our Keds sneakers as we indiscriminately tramped across him. During the eighteenth century in which Nathan had lived, smallpox wiped out much of New England's population, including an extremely high number of Native Americans. To come in contact with an infected individual or even their clothing and bedding was thought to be extremely contagious, even after death. That is why such an obviously well-thought-of fellow had come to rest in such an out-of-the-way place. A few farmers probably threw him in a hastily dug, shallow hole and ran like hell holding their breath.

It was with this sense of awe and privilege that we made regular pilgrimages to join him for a night of ghost stories and nervous sleep. Bruce had a floorless two-man pup tent that we always brought for the occasion. Really, it was little more than a piece of canvas folded over a center pole with flaps that tied closed at each end. We pitched the tent so that the headstone was actually inside it at one end. Kind of a headboard of sorts.

We usually spent much of the night speculating on what sort of gentleman Nathan Whitney might have been, and whether the carved face that stared at us from the top of the headstone was an accurate likeness of the man himself. If so, we thought, what a kindly soul he must have been. I wish we could have known him.

I moved from Boxborough before I had children of my

own, so I never passed on the secret to anyone. My young friends, as most of that generation did, also moved away to larger towns, big cities, and generally more exciting places with town centers. There were only a handful of friends who even knew about Nathan Whitney, as we were quite careful not to disclose such a closely guarded confidence by allowing just anyone to find out about it.

Today, Boxborough is a somewhat normal town. Still quite small, to be sure, but not one that would be described as particularly backward or behind the times. The sprawl of suburbs and condo complexes has overtaken much of the pastures and deep woods of my boyhood town, and commuters regularly make the trip to Boston and back daily. There are now quite a few businesses of varying description, including several gas stations, a pizza shop, a bank, a dry cleaner's, Chinese take-out, and a disturbing number of liquor stores. There's even a Holiday Inn on the outskirts by the interstate.

In a recent return trip from the neighboring state in which I now make my home, I drove to the graveyard where I had once spent an exhilarating, if not somewhat unnerving, night. I was pleased to see that it looked surprisingly the same as I remembered it. I walked the rutted paths between the ancient headstones and stopped at the entrance to the tomb bearing the large date, "1901." I tried to open the heavy iron door to peer in, as I have always harbored the distinct suspicion that I left my flashlight inside, but the door has since been welded shut, sealing forever in total blackness whatever remains inside.

Getting back into my car, I headed west from the cemetery, wondering if I'd be able to identify the curve on Burroughs Road where I used to climb the wall and hike into the dense woods to visit Nathan Whitney's grave. Things often look very different from a moving car than they do on foot, so I slowed considerably as I traveled the stretch that I was sure I would recognize.

I did not recognize anything. Where over forty years ago, dense, spooky woods closed in on both sides of the narrow road, now giant houses with three-car garages sprawled over nearly its entire length. Every bend of the road felt foreign and unfamiliar. My childhood landmarks of old stone walls, giant oak trees, a slight dip in the road here, a break in the wall there, had been supplanted by massive, pillared homes with manicured lawns.

I imagined Nathan Whitney's grave to have been callously bulldozed by some unscrupulous developer in the name of progress and profit. I was saddened to think that there would be nothing to prevent such a desecration, given that it was virtually unknown in the first place. Or perhaps the tiny stone had gone totally unnoticed as the wide blades of smoke-spewing machinery had plowed the powdery bones of Mr. Whitney under what is now the tastefully decorated recreation room of an oversized colonial.

Burroughs Road was once simply a way to get from one desolate end of town to the other. Nothing of significance lay along its winding route. Now there were whole new neighborhoods everywhere with new streets and cul-de-sacs leading to landscaped lots. Streets with new, trendy-sounding names like Coolidge Farm Road, Mayfair Drive, and... what's this? *Whitney Lane?*

I turned the car around and approached from the opposite direction. Everything looked so different, but this would have been about the spot where, years ago, I would have begun my trek into the woods. I turned onto Whitney Drive and proceeded at a crawl through the well-kept neighborhood. It seemed likely that if they had named a street for him, perhaps Nathan Whitney lies yet undisturbed at the very spot in which he was laid to rest nearly 250 years ago.

I pulled into the driveway of an elegant home and walked over neatly laid cobblestones to the front door, rehearsing what I would say if someone answered. An instant later a hesitant young woman with a toddler in tow held the door partially open.

"Excuse me for intruding," I began in my most polite voice. "I'm trying to locate the grave of a man that I believe might be buried in this neighborhood. Actually, if it still exists, he should be right in your backyard."

The door opening narrowed to a small crack as she nudged the child safely behind her.

"Do you know if there's anyone named Nathan Whitney buried around here?" I continued.

"No. I don't know anyone by that name," she insisted.

"Well, you probably wouldn't know him," I chuckled.

"He's been dead for over two hundred... " The door closed the rest of the way before I could finish the sentence.

After knocking on another door at which no one appeared, I proceeded to a third house where I was greeted by an exuberant black Lab and a boy of about ten who informed me that his mother was in the shower. When I explained what I was looking for and that he might be able to help me, he enthusiastically joined me on the front steps in his bare feet and pointed across the road to a small patch of undergrowth. "It's right there, Mister," he said. "It's in the middle of those trees."

Eyes widened, I thanked him heartily, and after being nearly pushed off the steps by his overly friendly canine companion, I went to take a look. Only twenty feet from the pavement, nes-tled in a shady grove of saplings, I spotted an upright, dark piece of slate. I approached to find that the spot had been encircled by a tidy stone enclosure of modest propor-tions. Heartened by such an obvious dis-play of reverence, I pushed away a low-hanging branch to

find staring back at me the familiar and kindly face of a man wearing a powdered wig.

I traced the carved letters with my finger, remembering nights spent in the shadow of its gray profile. I had found Nathan Whitney. And in so doing I had gained newfound admiration for those who had not only preserved this tiny fragment of history, but out of respect, had named a street in tribute to a man whose life and times we can only imagine.

Standing on that spot, I felt a connection to the past. Not only to my own childhood, but to a past that stretched back hundreds of years. At the same time, I also felt a strong

connection to the future. I found it comforting to know that even as the haunts of my youth are becoming unrecognizable, there are those who, at least for the time being, are succeeding in keeping some things the same, fulfilling an obligation to preserve the past for future generations.

After several moments, I stood and walked back to my car. In some ways, it felt like a completion. Over the past few decades, when the secret grave had occasionally come to mind, I had wondered if it was still there, and who, if anyone, knew about it. Although the location is no longer as clandestine as in my youth, which, at the time, I must say, evoked a certain captivating attraction, I left having seen the concern with which it has been carefully, though some-what more publicly preserved.

And with that, I drove slowly away, leaving behind what remains of Mr. Whitney to inspire the curiosity of another generation to reflect on the past and imagine what sort of person the man in the powdered wig might have been.

When Indians Misbehave

Whenever the Indians got out of line, Mrs. Cooke, our elderly next door neighbor, would be forced to take drastic action. This happened with frequent regularity, and it got so that we could predict when the eighty-five-year-old widow was about to take corrective measures. It didn't take me long to figure out that this would be one of those days. Stepping from her back door, Mrs. Cooke paused at a pansy-filled window box to pinch off a few dead leaves. She did not, however, let the leaves fall to the ground, but instead, placed them in the small pocket of the light blue cardigan sweater that was her signature outfit even on the hottest summer days. Not more than four feet from the window box, she stopped again at the end of her porch to carefully unwrap a small American flag that had been twisted around its tiny pole by the wind. Satisfied that all was in proper order, she turned her attention toward the task at hand—the Indians—and stepped from her back porch, placing one arm through the straps of her black leather purse. It was one of those generic, old-lady purses that all women over eighty are issued and required to carry with them at all times. The kind with the fake gold clasp and indestructible handles designed to last for ten years, or the rest of their life, whichever comes first.

With one arm slightly extended to steady herself as if resting on an imaginary cane, Mrs. Cooke made her way across the driveway past the neat borders of marigolds toward her tidy one-car garage. A few minutes after lifting the heavy door and entering the garage, she backed from its narrow confines in her 1951 Pontiac, her silver hair rising only slightly above the enormous steering wheel. Once safely clear of the garage, Mrs. Cooke emerged from the car and walked completely around it, paying particular attention to each wheel. Then, after pulling on the rope to close the garage door, she executed, as she always did, a tedious twelve-point turn in her driveway in order to inch out into the street headfirst, like someone timidly testing the water with one toe before finally making the commitment to take the plunge. She seemed oblivious to the possible presence of other vehicles, as if claiming the section of street directly in front of her house as her own personal stretch of pavement onto which others were not permitted.

Mrs. Cooke's Pontiac was a magnificent automobile. It had belonged to her late husband, Walter, and looked as if it had never attained speeds in excess of forty miles per hour. The back seat had been used only to transport an occasional bag of groceries, and due to her short, infrequent trips, it went for months on a tank of gas. Mrs. Cooke's car was painted in a stylish two-tone combination—a rich, deep ivory not unlike the color of her own teeth, and a beautiful, complimentary green that looked like the algae on Mr. Erikson's pond. As a child, I always liked Pontiacs because of the Indian logo. There was an Indian's profile embossed on each hubcap, but I particularly liked the one on the front of the hood. It was here that a streamlined sweep of chrome terminated in the shape of an Indian's head formed out of amber plastic the color of orange Life Savers candy. At night, the Indian's face lit up with a beautiful glow from a tiny light embedded within the plastic. It was because of this singular feature that I promised myself that when I grow up I would one day own a Pontiac, or at least the hood ornament.

As Mrs. Cooke headed off, the big sedan looked like a driverless car, a headless horseman rolling down the street at an exhilarating speed of fifteen miles per hour. A compressed crush of cars quickly formed behind her, and I watched until the big Pontiac rounded a bend at the end of the street, picking up momentum, and accelerating to a cruising speed of, perhaps, twenty-five. I watched until the last of the slow parade was finally out of sight.

I knew Mrs. Cooke would not be gone for long. Her routines were entirely predictable, and she seemed to repeat the identical movements with each performance. Like when she placed her single trash barrel at the edge of the curb every Monday morning at seven o'clock. You could almost set your watch by it. Because it was too heavy for her to lift, she scuffed the container the length of the driveway to the street. Once in place, she took the paper towel she had used to grab its handle and used it to wipe the sides of the barrel in spots where she believed it might have become soiled. Or maybe she just couldn't bring herself to throw away anything that had not been properly used up, and took the opportunity to do so. Then she'd lift the lid and gently place the used paper towel on top of the trash inside the barrel as if she were placing a cherry on top of a sundae. Finally, she'd carefully replace the lid, turn the barrel so that the handle was facing the street, and head back into the house.

About every other day, she also tended to a small bird feeder outside her kitchen window, repeating a series of well-practiced actions. Placing a plastic canister of birdseed on a ledge near the window, she removed the top of the feeder. Then she swept the empty husks from the feeder tray into a small container of some sort, being careful not to contaminate the grass below. During this part of the routine, I could sometimes see her mouth moving as if she were mildly reprimanding the finches for their lax dining habits. Then she poured in three scoops of seed from the plastic canister before replacing the top of the feeder. Always three scoops. Mrs. Cooke was a creature of habit.

Today's automobile ritual had become so familiar to my family that we had dubbed it "the Indian run." Her final destination was Laffin's Garage, an automotive repair shop not more than two miles away that specialized in servicing General Motors cars. The crew at Laffin's went through this familiar drill on a regular basis and understood exactly what was expected of them as the big sedan pulled into the lot. The long line of cars trailing Mrs. Cooke was finally able to pass and resume normal speed. Mrs. Cooke stepped from the old Pontiac as Sid Laffin held open the driver's side door.

"Morning, Mrs. Cooke. The Indians giving you trouble again?"

"I'm afraid so," came the concerned reply as Mrs. Cooke stood back to supervise the operation that was about to take place.

Even before Mrs. Cooke had stepped from her vehicle, Ernest, a young mechanic dressed in navy blue coveralls, had arrived carside holding a large screwdriver and a rubber mallet. Almost immediately, he began prying the left front hubcap from its rim. It had no sooner been removed, than he rotated the disk forty-five degrees and replaced it with a few well-placed blows of his mallet. Total elapsed time: ten seconds. He stood to walk to the other front wheel when Mrs. Cooke interjected, shaking her head with a look of bewilderment.

"I just don't understand," she puzzled. "They're fine every time I leave here. But by the time I get home, the Indians are all facing in different directions again. I just don't understand how that happens."

Over time, each mechanic had taken his turn at attempting to explain the mechanics of cornering and the dynamics of differential wheel rotation and their effects on the relative position of the Indian logos on each hubcap.

Had they been explaining the inherent benefits of a new technique for pruning rosebushes, she might have grasped what they were saying, but the laws of physics and simple mechanics was far beyond her comprehension. The boys at the garage, however, didn't mind going through this weekly drill, and indulged her with all the seriousness of rebuilding a transmission. When all four hubcaps had been aligned so that the Indians were all facing in the same direction, Mrs. Cooke was invited to walk around the car to ensure that the job had been properly completed. In fact, they insisted on it. They knew that by the time Mrs. Cooke reached home and pulled into her driveway, the bumps and turns in the road would once again have allowed the Indians to go their separate ways.

Sid never accepted payment for this service, and he held the car door open for Mrs. Cooke as she positioned herself in the front seat nearly disappearing behind the panoramic expanse of the dashboard. She then slipped the car into drive and began to move it slowly forward. She nodded to the entire crew who had now assembled to see her off. "Thank you, boys." She directed her comment to include Sid, even though he was probably in his fifties. They all waved in return. And with that, she was sent on her way like an ocean liner being launched down the slip-way on its maiden voyage.

I was still out in the yard when Mrs. Cooke returned after her brief round trip. I saw the big Pontiac round the bend in the road leading another slow procession of cars whose drivers rejoiced when she put on her blinker two hundred yards down the street and finally crept into her driveway. Rolling the big automobile to a stop a good twenty feet before it would have hit the garage, she emerged from its cavernous interior and walked ahead to lift the heavy garage door. Before she climbed back into her car, I watched with amused curiosity as she circumnavigated the vehicle. Looking down at each hubcap, she cocked her head, her silver hair sloping to one side, then the other. I could not see her face from where I stood in the backyard, but I imagined it to be that look one gets when trying to blow out those trick birthday candles that keep relighting.

After carefully returning the car to the garage and walking back out into the driveway, she turned to give it one prolonged look before pulling the rope to lower the garage door. Another futile attempt to control the Indians had already gone awry. I could not begin to guess at the number of times Mrs. Cooke had attended to this failed ritual, but wondered how many more it would take until she finally admitted defeat in her obsessive war with the Indians. She crossed the driveway and mounted the steps to her back door. The door had barely closed behind her when it reopened only a second later and Mrs. Cooke reappeared, still carrying her purse. She walked to the end of the porch and directed a final glance back toward the garage as if half-expecting to hear Indians laughing. Then, before turning to re-enter the house, she straightened her back, and lifted her chin as a way of displaying her resolve. And with the undaunted perseverance of an old woman who believed that even the laws of physics could be overcome with enough determination, she paused to unfurl the small American flag that had once again wrapped itself around its pole, and quietly disappeared back into the house.

My Oldest Friend

I was, perhaps, five when I first met my friend. We had just moved into town, and I was happy to have found someone in the neighborhood who seemed to genuinely enjoy spending time with me. Shortly thereafter, with no fanfare, and apparently little effort on his part, my friend did something of noteworthy accomplishment. He turned one hundred years old. The fact that my parents had repeatedly tried to impress upon me Mr. Mott's extreme age left me only vaguely aware that he was, perhaps, older than the oldest of the old. To a young child, however, surpassing in duration the span of a century had little meaning beyond the stooped frailty that was plainly evident.

Aside from the innate awareness that we were both at the extremities of our lives—me at the beginning, him at the end, we had little in common. The one thing we did share was a mutual but unspoken fascination with each others' age, though for quite different reasons. It was as if we were looking through opposite ends of a telescope. I was enthralled by the stories of an old man whose whole life was behind him. For Mr. Mott it was, perhaps, the vicarious anticipation of a young boy whose whole life lay ahead. Despite our obvious differences, the bond we shared should not have been at all surprising. He liked to talk. And I liked to listen.

Mr. Mott's presence seemed to command the attention of everyone around him, although, as far as I could tell, it was not the result of any action whatsoever on his part. Mr. Mott had only to show up and people would stop what they were doing to approach him. This was, perhaps, my first indication that there was something special, indeed magical, about the old man who seemed always to be around, yet seemed to come from nowhere. The worn, wooden cane that preceded every step bore a history of nicks and gouges, and seemed to be an outgrowth of his thin forearm. It terminated at a thick piece of rubber that made a dull thump on our wooden porch, making even the sound of his footsteps totally unique.

Mr. Mott's wardrobe was also distinctive. It perpetually consisted of a dark, threadbare suit, frayed at every edge, its elbows worn to a dull shine. The wrinkled pants fell far short of his scuffed shoes, allowing a good portion of his white socks to emphasize the gap. Between his curled-up lapels was a dingy, patterned necktie darkened in places by years of repeated handling. It hung limp from a thick and heavy knot loosely formed at the top that seemed to stretch under its own weight. But what made an impression on me more than the condition of his attire was the fact that it never varied. His one outfit became so familiar to me that in my mind it became an inseparable part of him. I can remember considering the possibility that he might have slept in it, but that was a question that, even at five years of age, I was not forward enough to ask. Despite its condition, the formality of dress together with his polite demeanor gave Mr. Mott an air of dignity long before I ever knew there was such a thing.

Mr. Mott, despite his feeble stature, incessantly walked the streets of West Acton, and frequently stopped as he passed our house if the opportunity for conversation presented itself. Being the eldest citizen in the entire town, Mr. Mott took it upon himself to find out all he could about newcomers, and having recently moved into the small Massachusetts community about twenty-five miles to the west of Boston, my family was of considerable interest to the self-appointed mayor. He leaned on his cane as he and my father discussed the old house we had just bought—a compact and tidy structure held together with wooden pegs that were plainly visible in the beams of the attic. The old man's keen interest in my father's plan to tear down part of the old building provided today's topic of energetic discussion.

I watched intently as the two figures engaged in animated conversation and gestured with arms outstretched toward the single-story wing that was being considered for demolition. Studying Mr. Mott from the side of our front yard, I wondered how someone so old could possibly have remained so small. At the dinner table I silently pondered the amount of time necessary to comprise one hundred years, a number I could barely count to, and a concept for which I had no context.

"Is he older than our car?"

"Yes," my father answered. "He's older than every car in the world."

"Is he older than... that chair?" I asked, looking around the dining room and pointing to the oldest looking thing I could see." About the only thing my father could think of that Mr. Mott was *not* older than was our house itself, which, despite being a relic from the mid-seventeen hundreds, did not seem to be as much on the verge of collapse as Mr. Mott.

I was never aware of the location of his own house. I could not, in fact, picture Mr. Mott in a house at all. Nor sitting at a dinner table, sleeping in a bed, or watching television like the rest of us. He seemed to exist only in a walking state. As if he were destined to spend eternity slowly retracing his steps along the town's quiet sidewalks. The only time I  ever saw my friend was when he was out on one of his strolls. Sometimes we'd spot the small, hunched-over figure some distance ahead when we were out driving in the car.

"There's Mr. Mott," whoever saw him first would say.

"He's over a hundred years old," my father would add as if providing some new piece of information no one had ever heard before.

Mr. Mott seemed always to be walking from one conversation to the next, stopping to talk to anyone who crossed his path. I always felt special when I was the one he was talking to. Mr. Mott had a way of making it seem as if I were the only person that mattered. Of course, he talked to whomever would listen. And to some who only pretended to listen. But I always felt as if he were telling me something that only I was privileged to hear. His quiet voice made everything sound like a secret. I listened attentively to his stories, unaware at the time that I was listening to a living history book. The memories he recalled were of a world that no longer existed. A world as foreign to me as any I could possibly imagine.

Born on Christmas Eve in the distant year of 1855, Otis Bailey Mott had lived in Acton since the age of nineteen. At various times throughout the long succession of decades he had been a farm worker, driven a butcher's meat wagon, and worked at the Hall Brothers Pail Company where he helped produce pails, tubs, and butter churns for the thriving trades of a growing town. He had been present during events that today seem like ancient history. At the time of his birth, Franklin Pierce was President, and California, where the gold rush was in full swing, had just

become the thirty-
first state. Lewis and
Clark's epic journey
exploring the hitherto
unknown western
reaches of the infant
country was still fresh
in the minds of many

Top right, Otis Bailey Mott at the Hall Brothers Pail Company

adults. Electric lights and the bicycle had yet to be invented. Had I been of an age to have possessed any appreciation
of history at all, I might have asked him what it was like to
live when Indians were still prevalent in parts of the country. I might have asked him about living through the presi-
dency of Abraham Lincoln and the end of slavery. He could
have told me firsthand about what it was like to have lived
through the Civil War, and how any war could have been
described as "civil." I could have arranged to bring Mr. Mott
to school for show and tell—a clever move that would have
gained me the favor of Mrs. McCarthy and the envy of my
classmates.

But my sense of the past was limited. My earliest memory was the birth of my sister, Kathy, an event that had
taken place a mere few years prior. History being an abstract
concept to a youngster, I was content to listen to whatever
Mr. Mott felt compelled to talk about. He recalled what the
town was like before the automobiles and the telephones
came. He'd point to a building or a parking lot or a patch of
grass and say, "That used to be a blacksmith shop," or "That

was where the first big steam locomotives used to stop on their way to Boston."

What he described was vastly different from what I saw around me. He evoked the details of the past with such vivid fondness that I wished I could visit the town he spoke about, finding it difficult to believe that I was already there. I was already standing on the very same ground where the people in his stories had come and gone years before. But I longed for a deeper connection to the past. I wanted tangible proof that I could hold in my hand and say, "Yes, those were real people, and they were right here."

That connection came the day my father began tearing down the long, wooden porch on the front of our old house, and it was Mr. Mott who helped provide that connection. It was the old man who suggested that I sift the dirt underneath the porch.

"That porch has been there for a very long time," he impressed upon me, "and a lot of people over the years must have dropped things down between those old floorboards by accident." He noted that because there was no access to the space under the porch, once items had fallen through its wide cracks, there would have been no way to retrieve them.

"Take a piece of screen from one of the old windows," he suggested, "and shake the dirt through it." He made a shaking movement with both arms that caused his old wooden cane to swing about wildly. "I bet you'll find lots of interesting old things down there."

He kept talking about something he called Indian head pennies, insisting that I would discover plenty of them. I didn't understand what an Indian's head had to do with money. But a penny was a penny, no matter how funny-sounding its name. And to me, a penny meant a gumball. Certainly ample reward for whatever sifting time would be required.

I don't remember discovering much of anything below the ancient porch floor except for a handful of handmade, square nails. It didn't matter. It was the activity itself that gave me my connection to the people who, in a former era, had walked just above where I diligently sifted the sediment one handful at a time. Knowing that the possibility for discovery existed was all I needed to connect me with the world of which Mr. Mott so often spoke.

Not long afterward at the age of one hundred and one, with no fanfare, and apparently little effort on his part, Mr. Mott once again did something quite noteworthy. He died. He left without answering so many of my questions. If only I had asked them. But he also left me with something very precious—an appreciation of history. For much of my childhood I tried to see my small town through his old eyes. The way he had described it to me many times. With a little practice and a lot of imagination, I was able to look past the telephone poles, the electric streetlights, the cars, and the modern buildings. I found I could block out the cement sidewalks and the paved streets in my mind. I was able to look at buildings that for most of my childhood housed variety stores, insurance agencies, and barber shops, mentally block out the big plate glass windows, and see harness makers and livery stables. I could imagine horses inside single-story wooden structures impatiently tamping the floor and pulling hay from nearby troughs. I could hear wagons clattering over bumpy roads and polite citizens strolling in front of tiny shops. And like a bookmark in time, I find I still use Mr. Mott's long life span as the mental measure of a century.

Considering the brief time that our existence overlapped, Mr. Mott left a disproportionate impression on me. The fact that my memories of him remain indelible over fifty years later is reason enough to keep them alive. Though Mr. Mott lived an extraordinarily long life, the true assessment of one's time here is not measured in duration. Nor is it what we are able to accumulate during our brief tenure that matters most. Mr. Mott had little. But he left much. Those who remember stopping on the sidewalk to listen to the words of an old man are the recipients of Mr. Mott's legacy. A story here, a bit of wisdom there, a kind word.

The official report states that Otis Mott died of cardiac failure, the attending medical examiner attesting to the fact that he was found "pulseless at wrists." That, however, is not the end of the story. While the official documents filed in the town records may never again have occasion to be read, my hope is that the words you now read will in some small way keep the memory of my friend alive in a way that a few letters and numbers carved into a granite marker cannot. He was not famous. He made no mark on what is generally considered by most to be history. But in a very profound way, Mr. Mott was much more than that. He was my friend.

A Lot on Your Plate

Playing the license plate game was easier when I was a child. It was a traditional family pastime whenever we would pile into our 1961 Chevy station wagon for more than an hour or so. We would collect sightings from as many different states as we could identify before arriving at our destination. Time was when you could I.D. a plate at a distance of several car lengths at sixty miles per hour.

"Yellow on black! There's California," Dad would call out.

"And there's blue and orange. Pennsylvania!" we'd all shout in unison.

In the front seat, Mom kept score on the back of a napkin or used envelope she'd found in the glove compartment. During dry spells, Dad would flex his knowledge of state capitals and geography. It was fun to imagine, for example, standing on the one place in the entire country where you could be in four different states at once. Someday, he promised, we'd drive to that spot on our way to the Grand Canyon.

"Minnesota," someone would call out as Mom added

another state to her written list. Then Dad would add, "Did you know that, not counting the newly added state of Alaska, Minnesota is the northernmost state?"

Our little game was a fun way to learn about different states. I remember paying close attention to cars from particularly far-away states, expecting their inhabitants to look, I don't know, somehow different than families in our own state.

We in the back seat were at a definite disadvantage, but it was a team sport and individual achievement didn't seem to matter as much as the group tally. In recent years, however, the degree of difficulty as well as the frustration level for our travel pastime has been raised considerably. That fact became increasingly evident on a recent road trip from New England to the midwest as my wife and I, along with our two children, tried to revive the old family activity.

It seems that sometime between JFK and Y2K, a quiet shift on our asphalt playing field had occurred. The trademark color schemes of state license plates had given way to a dizzying array of colors and artwork. Most states now offer drivers so many image choices that today our little travel game must be played at close range. The once familiar highway signatures of proud states—instantly recognizable old friends—now change colors like a fickle shopper trying on different hats.

Our neighboring state of Massachusetts, for example, offers images of a whale, a rainbow trout, a lighthouse, a children's drawing, the Boston Red Sox logo, the Boston

Bruins logo, the Olympics logo, an American flag, an old mill scene, and a dog and cat design. That's in addition to red on white as well as blue on white lettering. Same state, twelve different designs.

Identification of state plates became such a challenge that to avoid tailgating, we soon found ourselves waiting until we had slowed for tollbooths to even attempt a search. It felt like cheating when we added eight sightings simply by driving around the Niagara Falls parking lot.

Back on the road, our anticipation would rise whenever we'd spot an unfamiliar plate and we'd rush to catch up for a closer look. Often we'd discover it was a state we had already counted, just a different design.

Whenever our game stalled for lack of new sightings, the claims and hyperbole of state mottos provided a good topic for discussion. Geography, history, and trivia all in one concise phrase.

Both Ohio ("Birthplace of Aviation") and North Carolina ("First in Flight"), for example, seem to be making the same claim to history. Actually, both mottos are accurate. Because of its favorable wind patterns, Kittyhawk, North Carolina, was the site chosen for the Wright brothers' maiden voyage. But it was Wilbur and Orville's Ohio bicycle shop where the plans for aircraft were developed.

Wisconsin ("America's Dairyland"), on the other hand, seems content to let Minnesota's boast of "10,000 Lakes" go unchallenged, even though, according to a brochure we picked up there, the lakes in Wisconsin number *fifteen thousand.*

The motto from my own state of New Hampshire, however, is in a category by itself. In its infinite wisdom, New
Hampshire has waived the opportunity to use its motto for
purposes of promoting much-needed tourism. Instead, the
state requires any resident wishing to drive a car to do so
while displaying the dubious creed, "Live Free or Die." I find
it a somewhat embarrassing political statement to be forced
to promote. It also seems to be an ironically cruel joke on
the inmates at the state prison for men in Concord who,
according to the official I spoke to there, stamp out more
than 400,000 of the plates each year.

Actually, in 1973, the State Supreme Court ruled that
it is perfectly legal for drivers to cover up that portion of
their license plate displaying the state motto. So citizens
may now enjoy the privilege of owning a car without also
having to assert their morbid preference for death over
whatever's in second place.

But while the mottos may hold some passing interest for
a few, they are mostly seen (or more likely ignored) for what
they are. Blatant propaganda designed to lure motoring
tourists for a visit. And, despite remaining unchanged for
decades, the mottos remain ultimately forgettable. How
many travelers would know which state brags of being "The
Peace Garden State"? Or how about "The Natural State"?
And if asked, could you recall the mottos for West Virginia,
Michigan, or, say, Nevada?

Recent technology, however, has now made it cost-effective to print full-color images on metal, making it possible for polite, interstate rivalries to escalate into fully illustrated, four-lane public relations wars. License plates have become the shameless domain of advertising, and unwitting drivers the bearers of colorful state messages.

Images that look more like pages from children's books are hard to ignore, and the lack of instant recognition forced us to pass and re-pass the same cars several times. "Is that a picture of a tiger on that plate?" We'd strain to read the state names under strange, colorful imagery of birds, flowers, and a host of nature scenes. (By the way, the tiger, as we discovered on the third pass, is one of Pennsylvania's offerings.)

Despite the frustration of difficult identification, some of the new plates are quite interesting. We started giving our own awards for plates we felt deserved some special recognition.

The Prettiest—Arizona with a very colorful desert scene.

The Busiest—Texas which managed to cram onto one plate, the space shuttle, the moon, the stars, a cowboy on horseback, an oil well, and a tumbleweed.

A drab grey and white plate received our award for *The Worst Design*—Sorry, Rhode Island, but that's the ugliest ocean wave we've ever seen.

We found no imagery on the plates from Vermont. (Not surprising for a state that outlaws billboards.) In fact, the plain white numbers on green is as I remember it from childhood. It was actually refreshing to know that there is at least one state apparently resisting the trend toward designer plates. It actually sends a subliminal message of how unchanged and unspoiled, in fact, the state itself is.

We also spotted the plate celebrated in Jan Harmon's obscure folk song, "The State o' Maine's License is the Only License with a Dead Animal on it." The animal, of course, a bright red lobster. Dead, because as everyone from New England knows, lobsters don't turn red until they're cooked.

Another frustrating aspect of the license plate game has nothing to do with the proliferation of colorful imagery. It's those cheap novelty frames proclaiming, "Proud To Be Union," or "Tri-State Auto Sales." Most are from car dealerships. Some tout sports teams or colleges. A few indicate drivers' personal interests or hobbies, just in case you were tempted to wave them over and start a conversation.

What makes these frames so frustrating is that many actually cover the name of the state, making it now possible to stand at arm's length behind a parked vehicle and have no idea where it's from. We caught up to countless vehicles displaying uniquely colored plates, only to be denied our payoff because the driver would rather have us know that, "I love my Golden Retriever."

Sometimes we'd venture a guess based on other clues. If a family has a license plate frame that reads "Green Bay Packers," and a kid in the back seat is wearing one of those foam rubber cheese hats, there's a good chance they're from Wisconsin. But that's only a guess.

At the rate things are going, license plates of the future will take information overload to a whole new level. Imagine an embedded magnetic strip similar to your credit cards. Every vehicle would be equipped with a device to automatically scan the strips as they fly by in the passing lane. A digital readout would appear on the screen of your car's control panel. No need to even glance over at them. You'll know instantly who just cut you off. "Hi. We're the Clarks. We're from Davenport, Iowa. Our child is an honor roll student at the middle school, we love the USA, and we'd rather be golfing."

Hey, why stop there? States could sell advertising space on the magnetic strips causing an embedded product message to flash onto your control screen. "Long, hot day on the road? Have an ice-cold Coke." Now add GPS technology and you'd really have something. The system would know exactly where you are on the highway, and could prepare you for the "Amish Farm Museum and Theme Park—Next Exit."

Most of the revenue from these embedded ad strips, of course, would go to state coffers, but the person who first suggests the new application for this technology could make a fortune.

A fortune... Hmmm... On second thought, forget you ever read this.

From the Dawn of TV
(Until about Noontime)

When I say there was nothing to watch on TV, that is
not an indictment of the quality of network programming.
I mean it quite literally. Every Saturday morning when I was
a kid, I came downstairs, still in my pajamas, to watch cartoons. As usual, I was ready and waiting even before those
in the broadcast industry had begun their day. Early TV
wasn't ahead of its time, but I was. In my eager anticipation,
I usually spent the first fifteen minutes or so sitting cross-
legged on the braided rug directly in front of the tiny screen,
fixated on a kind of magical, hypnotic hex sign that was
accompanied by a high-pitched hum and broadcast over the
airwaves to fill the void created by the absence of actual
programming. From a very early age I sensed something of a
mystical quality underlying this unsettling presence that
possessed our TV in this eerie state of unconsciousness.

Questioning grown-ups about the odd phenomenon
had shed little light on the mystery, and finding their weak
explanations completely lacking, I was left totally dissatis-
fied. Their usual response about the meaning of the strange
symbols on the screen was an indifferent "I don't know."

Other than the fact that the vacuous signal that possessed our TV was called a test pattern, there was little they could tell me about it. To my way of thinking, anything that adults did not understand qualified as a mystery of the highest order.

The omnipresent test pattern was something that I found disquieting, though oddly comforting. It was always there. Like the sun. If it had a purpose, it was beyond my understanding. Over time, I came to accept that it was ultimately not intended to be fully understood by children like myself. Having imbued our tiny TV set with vaguely human characteristics, I ultimately accepted its projection of the perplexing image merely as what the TV did while it (and I) was sleeping. I was somewhat aware that there were real people working unseen behind the whole television phenomenon, but exactly who and where they were and what they were doing was a mystery. Even more puzzling was why they wanted me to see this strangely captivating symbol. Experience had told me that it would not move or vary in any way from its maniacal, unblinking stare. Yet, there was no denying the fact that I could not avert my gaze from its transfixing drone. It had a strange and compelling power over me. I had considered the possibility that the powers behind the alien world of television, through their repeated use of the test pattern, were casting a spell on me, and that I would one day awaken to discover that I had grown an additional finger, or that I liked brussels sprouts. The fact that the image was broadcast so incessantly on something as defining as television gave it a significance that I could not begin to comprehend, but did not dare to underestimate.

The elements that comprised its vaguely occult theme were much too detailed and specific to have no meaningful purpose. Yet, it seemed impossible that I would ever resolve my curiosity by pointing these features out to an adult since, by the time my parents had awakened and come downstairs, the image had vanished from view leaving no visible trace with no apparent way to retrieve it.

The strange symbolism of its design only added to its mystique. Mesmerizing energy rays emanated like spokes from a central point and terminated at a large wheel on which a series of cryptic numbers was arranged in a very precise pattern. This was undoubtedly a code of some sort, but until I had reached the age where I would study arithmetic

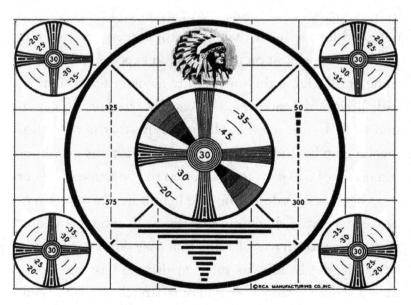

in school, even the simplest numbers would retain their unfathomable complexity. Smaller versions of the wheel occupied each corner, and the entire design was overlaid onto an exacting grid pattern. The entire symbol looked like something that might have been beamed down from outer space had it not been for the presence of a puzzling image at the top center. Directly above the large, central wheel was a picture of an Indian chief, wearing a full headdress. I could only guess at his identity and significance, but he was almost certainly a key to deciphering the riddle. Had all of this been lying flat on a table, it might have passed for a board game or ouija board of some sort. But being vertically displayed on television, this seemed a highly unlikely possibility.

I moved even closer to the TV until I was directly in front of the screen. Although my parents had told me it was not good for me to sit that close, the screen was tiny and you had to be almost on top of it if you expected to see anything at all. Being the only family member up at such an early hour of the morning, I repeatedly acted on a compulsion to look over my shoulder to ensure that nothing was sneaking up behind me. Out of the corner of my eye, I was certain that I had detected motion in the direction of a floor lamp by the closet door. The pale light from the test pattern cast exaggerated shadows onto the walls, and I stared at them long enough to make sure that they did not move. On occasion, the headlights of a car driving past the house caused an elongated panel of light to stretch across the ceiling and crawl down the living room curtain. Through all of this, the test pattern continued its eerie vigil.

The transfixing monotony of the test pattern might have been even more disturbing had it not been for the fact that after staring at it for an extended period of time, it was eventually replaced by cartoons. Upon this most welcome transition, the television awakened from its comatose state by abruptly generating high-energy, animated characters that burst onto the screen with funny voices, lively music, and exaggerated, over-the-top sound effects. Sitting alone in the still-dark living room, however, I sensed that the schizophrenic energy behind the mysterious test pattern was somehow still lurking, perhaps even responsible for, Roadrunner and Sylvester the cat. Its penetrating stare had fixated on me much too long to have simply vanished, and it often took several lively cartoons to fully dissipate the residual energy of its haunting trance.

By the time daylight had broken and my parents had come downstairs, I was fully engrossed in *Bugs Bunny*. All lingering traces of the eerily frightening test pattern had been dissolved away by my laughter and by Mom's activity in the kitchen as she made breakfast. As creepy as the test pattern could be, it was always positively associated with Saturday mornings—a time when I was allowed to watch *Mighty Mouse, Tom and Jerry,* and a host of other animated shorts in uninterrupted succession. The spooky cryptogram became a familiar icon associated with my early childhood along with Howdy Doody, the Quaker Oats box, and a Davy

Crockett hat that continued to make occasional appearances at the back of my closet long after it had outlived its usefulness as an article of apparel.

After breakfast I was sometimes allowed to watch a little more TV, but eventually, my parents insisted that I turn it off and go play with my friends. I usually went straight to John Veasie's house where his mother let him watch TV until almost noontime. There was also another reason to watch TV at John's house. The Veasie's had a device that transformed their black and white television into a color TV. This, at a time when color broadcasts did not exist. The device consisted of a rigid piece of transparent plastic that was affixed to the front of the TV screen. The plastic was divided into three equal horizontal bands of color—blue at the top, fading to beige in the middle, and green at the bottom. At a time when television programming was predominantly westerns consisting typically of prairie landscape scenes, the plastic filter worked quite well. It didn't work so well for shots like the inside of a sheriff's office where the Lone Ranger and Tonto's faces were inexplicably blue and they stood knee-deep in what looked like a greenish swamp. But we were willing to stretch the boundaries of reality for the thrill of watching "color" TV even before it had been invented. We rarely watched a show in its entirety because we were constantly switching channels between *The Roy Rogers Show* and *Wild Bill Hickock* looking for landscape scenes that most closely conformed to the colorized overlay.

It would be several years before any shows were broadcast in color. And even then, it didn't happen overnight. The first few programs shown in color were announced with much fanfare. Preceding such shows on NBC, for example, an animated peacock spread its tail feathers as they turned from gray into a spectrum of bright colors. A harp crescendo accompanied an announcer's voice as he proudly proclaimed, "The following program is brought to you in living color on NBC." On our TV, the peacock's plumage fanned out magnificently, but remained perpetually gray.

Our vintage television set was an RCA Victor. This pleased me greatly because I always thought RCA had the best logo. It was a dog named "Nipper" who cocked his head at "The sound of his master's voice." Of course, this was a holdover from the days when RCA was Radio Corporation of America and they made only radios, but still, no other company's logo even came close.

Our old RCA was enormously large for the size of its nearly round screen that measured only seven inches across. It was like peering into the window of a clothes dryer and seeing Ed Sullivan. An antenna known as rabbit ears sat atop the bulky box and required adjusting depending on what channel you were watching, or if the wind was blowing the trees outside, and where people in the room were positioned. This appendage, as I recall, eventually gave way to a more effective configuration of heavy-gauge wire that my dad wrapped with Reynolds aluminum foil at both ends and stretched between our two living room windows.

An impressive array of dials across the front of the set gave one a sense of amazing control over this new technology. Among the selection of knobs, the two that were most often used were labeled "horizontal hold" and "vertical hold." With great frequency, and for no apparent reason, the TV picture would flip from top to bottom or from side to side as if a picture book whose pages were all identical was flipping from one page to the next. This irritating phenomenon could be remedied only by the delicate touch of a trained hand. Turn the knob too far and the picture would begin flipping in the opposite direction. Occasionally, the picture would flip only halfway and get stuck. When this happened, an annoying, heavy black bar would split the screen in two so that the bottom half of the picture appeared on the top half of the screen, and the top of the picture was at the bottom. Even when the picture was not jumping around, it was often snowy and full of static. This could sometimes be fixed by adjusting the antenna in combination with a large ring around the channel selector knob called the fine-tuning adjustment. All of this gave me the impression that there must be a very high degree of difficulty in getting any picture at all to appear on a box in one's living room. My gratitude for this, however, far outweighed my annoyance at its occasional poor quality.

The housing of the TV itself was a marvel to behold. Since television sets had not previously existed, and America did not really know what a TV was supposed to look like, their manufacturers thought it would be a great idea to make them look like huge radios with a window. More expensive and larger models were actually advertised as furniture, and magazine ads pictured the bulky sets as the focal point of modern living rooms. Happy families watched from trendy, sectional sofas, Dad in his suit and tie, smoking a pipe, and Mom in high heels and full makeup wearing a fancy dress.

Our set, while not what one would classify as furniture, was generously enhanced with heavy brown plastic that was intended to fool people into thinking it was wood. The portion that enclosed the speaker was covered with a course beige fabric embedded with gold metallic threads that sparkled when light hit them. Small pieces of decorative metal trim that looked as if they might have come from the dashboard of a car added the final stylish touch.

Around the back of the set was another story. The back of the set was all business. No attempt had been made to dress up this side of the box, and it was clear that the TV was not intended to be viewed from this angle. Perforations in a cheap, but sturdy fiberboard cover allowed one to peer inside at the array of glass tubes that glowed a dim orange when the set was on. But what I remember most about the back of the set was the smell. It smelled electrical and hot. It smelled dangerous. A paper warning label affixed to the fiberboard cover added to the peril and was quite enough to prevent me from doing too much exploring back there. Besides, all the fun stuff was happening up front.

When the TV was switched off, the picture collapsed

into a progressively smaller point of light in the center of the dark screen that resembled a faint star fading away in the heavens. I always tried to delay my bedtime by a couple of minutes by asking to watch the white dot until it disappeared completely from view. It took a surprisingly long time to totally vanish, and even then, I tried to delay the inevitable by pushing my face right up to the screen, insisting that I could still see it.

Television, not unlike myself, was in its formative years. Three stations provided the only viewing choices. On the bulky channel dial of our RCA Victor set, numbers 4, 5, and 7 were the only selections at which viewers would find something to watch. And then, only at certain hours each day. Programming began in the morning and went off the air late at night, ending with the national anthem accompanied by a film of an American flag waving in the breeze. This patriotic tribute was followed by a man's voice identifying the station and announcing that the day's broadcast was now concluding. I was rarely up late enough to witness the signing-off ceremony, but on occasion when my grandmother was babysitting, I managed to watch it by convincing her that Mom and Dad let me stay up late all the time.

After the last waning strains of the Star-Spangled Banner had faded away, the high-pitched hum and maniacal stare of the test pattern began its night-long vigil. The reappearance of the nightmare-inducing hex sign signalled that another day had come full-circle. Once again, I puzzled about the identity of the Indian chief and wondered about his significance. I turned to my grandmother who was already beginning to doze off. I pointed to the mysterious symbols and complex numeric codes and asked, "But, Grammy... What does all that mean?"

Of all the people I ever asked, my grandmother was the only one who ever gave me a definitive answer for deciphering the mystery of its meaning. She stood and walked directly up to the odd arrangement of cryptic symbols, paused a moment, then immediately turned off the set. As the picture faded to an ever-shrinking white dot at the center of the screen, she turned to me and clapped her hands together.

"It means it's time for bed."

Digging Up the Past

Buried beneath an unmarked site at a specific convergence of latitude and longitude lies a small Egyptian relic of considerable worth. In my early teens, I saw a picture of the object in a book given to me as a Christmas present. The photo was of a handsome old coin bearing the likeness of an Egyptian man wearing an unusual headpiece—a fez, I think it's called—with a tassel that hung down on one side of his expressionless profile. The Egyptian man on the coin seemed serious and distant, and completely unaware of how comical his fez would appear to a modern American teenager—A lampshade on a party-goer's head. A bucket of Kentucky Fried Chicken overturned in a slapstick movie.

Though the book pictured many other coins, everything about this particular coin underscored its foreignness. Its design included hieroglyphic-like symbols, reminders of a far-away culture of mummies and pyramids. Underneath the photo in the book was a description of the coin and a caption that read in part, "... rare and desirable coin. Obtainable only with the greatest of difficulty."

The fact that I am the only individual on the planet

who happens to know the exact location of this buried treasure should not be surprising considering that I am the one who buried it.

Before I continue, I must note that the caption in the book is not entirely accurate. You see, I encountered no difficulty whatsoever in its acquisition. It came to me, in fact, quite effortlessly as one of a handful of coins given to me by a woman I never met. Having professed an interest in coin collecting when I was about twelve, an elderly acquaintance of my grandmother, who was in the midst of the tedious process of reducing her accumulation of worldly possessions, decided that I might be of some help in accomplishing this goal.

It was serendipitous that such a fine collection should come my way, although my appreciation was limited merely to what happened to catch my eye. The criteria for my meager collection was measured by curiosity with little regard to monetary value. The less a coin resembled what my friends might find in their pockets, the more I wanted it. I once spent two weeks' allowance for one coin merely because it was octagonal with a hole in the middle. Another coin found its way into my collection solely by virtue of the fact that it came from Russia. The early 1960s was the height of the cold war, and my friends and I had a morbid fascination with anything associated with the country that had threatened to wipe us off the face of the earth.

The particular Egyptian coin that I buried was one of my favorites due to the fact that it happened to be pictured in my coin book. Of the hundreds of possible coins to select for inclusion in the scant chapter devoted to Egypt, I thought it highly unlikely that the very coin I held in my hand should be featured. Every detail, including the date, was exactly identical. And unlike many of my coins that had been worn so smooth as to render the date indistinguishable, the Egyptian piece was pristinely crisp in every detail. The tassel on the man's headpiece clearly showed each strand, and the lettering stood out in sharply etched relief.

Ordinarily, I might have found myself daydreaming about where the coin had been over the course of its lifetime—in the pocket of a camel driver or in the tight clutch of a little boy passing the entrance to King Tut's tomb on his way to an Egyptian sidewalk bazaar to buy candy. But I knew that none of these images would have been accurate. This coin had not been in general circulation, and had, perhaps, never been spent. Even as an adolescent, I was mindful of the classification of coinage by its condition—fair, good, very good, fine, uncirculated, mint, and so on. I was aware that I was one of a very few ever to have held this coin.

I can offer no excuse other than ignorance or childish intrigue for its eventual interment. However, it was not buried on a whim. Rather, it was deposited with great ceremony. I placed it inside a finely crafted wooden box lined with purple velvet that had been designed to hold silver flatware service for eight. The kind with slots for knives, forks, and spoons. I then wrapped the box in something that I presumed to be waterproof and buried the entire package to a depth of perhaps ten or twelve inches. I don't know if I ever intended to go back to reclaim the coin. I like to think that I would certainly have drawn a treasure map for its eventual recovery had this been the case. I would envision myself decades later unfurling the now brittle and dog-eared parchment of cryptic symbols detailing its exact where-abouts. Forty paces at a thirty degree angle from the stone wall, past the woodshed, turn left at the apple tree, and another six paces in the direction of the big split boulder. But in the absence of any such documentation, I am left to wonder about my intention.

Two things keep me from unearthing this treasure. The first is a matter of practicality. Though the location of the treasure is in the middle of a grassy field in back of my childhood home, it is now the grassy field in back of some-one else's home, and I doubt they would condone me defac-ing their property with test holes in my exotic quest. You see, while I remember where I buried the treasure, the accu-racy of my recollection would place it only within about forty feet or so of the precise spot. The rest would be trial and error digging. Forty paces past the woodshed. Or was it Sixty? Is that twelve-year-old's paces, or adult paces? A short distance from the apple tree. Where's the apple tree? Oh my God! The apple tree is gone! I could, perhaps, come close to the spot by a vague recognition of subliminal landmarks—the slope of the land, the general proximity of the stone wall. But, really, it was a long time ago, and things always look different when you go back and visit childhood haunts.

The second reason for not initiating my archeological dig is of a more tactical nature. Even if the present landowners were to allow me to dig for my treasure, they wouldn't just let me walk away with it. What would be in it for them? And if my hunt proved successful, I wouldn't want to give the relic away to strangers. What would be in it for me? No, if I were going to unearth the coin, I would need to go in the middle of the night led by the dim flicker of a lantern. Like a khaki-clad adventurer. Like a grave robber. But what about the sound? The clanking of the shovel in the stony soil would surely wake them.

I suppose I would have to sneak into the backyard while the homeowners were on vacation. They'd never have to know, and they might attribute the newly created system of trenches to a migrating community of gophers. You know, one of those traveling colonies that appears overnight and then mysteriously disappears. But what about the neighbors? When I buried the treasure, it was out of sight from inquisitive residents. There was only a sparse scattering of homes in the area at the time, and it was easy to find secret hiding places. So isolated was our stretch of narrow road that the houses on either side of our own were in different towns.

But now... now there would certainly be new homes

that had been built in the interim, turning what had been a remote section of country into something approximating a suburb. New near-mansions with their three-car garages are springing up everywhere almost overnight. Like gopher colonies. What would these new families of young professionals think if they were to look out their faux antique, leaded glass windows to see a lone figure creeping into their neighbor's yard with a shovel and a lantern? The possibility of midnight gardening would seem improbable. More likely, their imaginations would run to more clandestine activities such as exhuming a body. Or burying one. Unearthing a long-lost Egyptian treasure, while romantic, would be much further down the list.

I don't know exactly what I'd do if I found the coin. The possibility seems remote at best. I'm not even certain that I'd want to find it.

There's a scene from the 1971 movie, *Harold and Maude*, in which young Harold, played by Bud Cort, professes undying love for the seventy-nine year old Maude, played by Ruth Gordon. While the two are sitting one evening on a dock at the edge of a harbor, Harold gives Maude a coin from an arcade that he has had engraved. In a tender and poignant moment, Maude admires the coin, reading the inscription, *"Harold loves Maude."* She holds it to her heart, exclaiming, "This is the nicest gift I've received in years," and then flings it into the bay. Aghast, Harold looks to Maude for an explanation. With genuine and loving sentiment, she turns to him and says, "Now I'll always know where it is."

Even if, against all odds, I were to somehow dig up the coin, and even if I were allowed to retain possession, I would not sell the treasure. I would undoubtedly lock it away in a strongbox. Out of sight. Safe where no one would find it. Just as it is now. Come to think of it, perhaps that was my intention from the very beginning.

Santa Claus vs. the Tooth Fairy

I explored the newly created gap in my smile by sticking my tongue partially through the narrow opening while my teeth were still clenched tightly together. For the next several weeks I would enjoy the temporary distinction of being able to squirt water from my mouth in a perfectly formed trajectory over what I hoped would be an enviable distance. After one last, careful inspection of the harvested tooth, I gently wrapped it in a Kleenex, folding it in half, then in half again. I then tucked it under my pillow with the assurance that by morning it would have made the miraculous transformation into a shiny, new dime. At some point in the middle of the night, the Tooth Fairy would float into my second-story bedroom and, without a sound, make the switch.

Okay, that's not the way it happened at all. There was nothing mysterious about the appearance of money where formerly there had been only a used and now-useless tooth. I knew all along that shortly after I was asleep, or pretended to be, one of my parents would not float, but tiptoe into my room to remove the tiny package leaving ten cents in its place. Not until I had lost all of my baby teeth, however, did I let on that I never really believed in the Tooth Fairy. I don't believe I ever confessed to even a hint of skepticism, a risky move that would have put in jeopardy my ten cents per lost tooth—a considerable sum of money in those days. Besides, my parents seemed to enjoy playing make-believe, and I didn't want to spoil their fun.

There was precious little to justify one's belief in the Tooth Fairy. I mean, when you think about it, what do we really know about her? There was never a concerted effort to shed light on the details of her alleged existence. There was no North Pole equivalent for the Tooth Fairy. Where did she come from and where did she go? There was never a plausible explanation given for her sudden appearance in children's bedrooms or her mildly freakish tooth fetish. There was no holiday based on her benevolence toward the children of the world. No pictures. No songs. No depart-ment store lines of kids waiting to sit on her lap and pull her wings to see if they were real. In light of her negligible pub-licity and the lack of details surrounding her life, there was little to make a convincing argument for her existence, even to a seven-year-old. There was simply too much left unexplained. Besides, what use could she possibly have for all of those discarded teeth that, by now, would have num-bered in the millions? And where did she get all of the money to leave under kids' pillows? Was she selling our teeth to get the money? And if so, to whom? And what were *they* doing with all of our teeth? The whole thing just seemed too far-fetched. But I kept my gap-riddled mouth shut so as not to jeopardize the easy income. I didn't ask questions because I didn't want my parents to have to answer and admit that it was all a childish hoax.

"Well, now that you don't believe," I could hear them rationalize, "there's no reason to pay you. We'll just take the money we would have given you and buy more cod liver oil or brocolli."

Perhaps the most disturbing question arising from the Tooth Fairy's alleged existence, however, was why she left me a dime per tooth, while she left Tommy McPhee across the street a whole quarter? From what I could determine, Tommy's teeth were not substantially more attractive than my own. In closely studying them once during a game of Go Fish, there appeared, in fact, to be no distinguishing features whatsoever, and certainly nothing that would cause his teeth to be more valuable. Of course, I never asked this question either because I already knew the answer. The only possible explanation was that there *was* no Tooth Fairy.

Once when I was in the second grade, my parents neglected to fulfill their covert obligation. I awoke to find my tooth still carefully wrapped in its tissue and tucked snugly under my pillow, and me no richer than when I had gone to sleep.

"Maybe she was really busy last night," they reasoned. "Or perhaps she didn't get the word that you had lost a tooth. Timely communication must be difficult," they continued, "what with her flitting all over the world and all.

Leave it under your pillow again tonight and maybe she'll come."

I did. She did.

The prospect of the Tooth Fairy being a complete figment of my parents' imagination, however, did not upset me. I did not feel deprived or cheated out of an inherent right of childhood. It wasn't as if I had once believed something and it suddenly turned out not to be true. Perhaps, if kids lost their teeth at age three, things would be different. But I *never* believed in the Tooth Fairy. So there was never the sensation of someone bursting my bubble. It wasn't as if Santa Claus had turned out not to be real. Of course, at the time, that would have been preposterous. I mean, there was just no comparison between the Tooth Fairy and Santa Claus. I considered myself quite mature and wise beyond my years that I was not convinced of the existence of an obviously fictional character like the Tooth Fairy. I was just too smart to have been taken in by the fabricated stories of a flying pixie who collected dispossessed dental extractions. Fairies were made up for little kids. That's why little kids' books are called "fairy tales." Because they're not real. By reserving my faith for the man in the red suit, I showed my discernment at being able to distinguish fact from fantasy— myth from reality.

Actually, a fifth grader had once tried to convince me that Santa Claus wasn't real. But Skippy McClay had a habit of telling lies. It was Skippy who told me that Mr.

Littlefield kept the skeleton of a dead dog in his cellar. He just wasn't a credible source.

"Santa Claus is just for little kids," he laughed, pointing at me as if I had just been tricked into eating a worm. "He's not a real person."

"Yes he is," I countered.

"Prove it," taunted Skippy.

That's when I knew I had him. We just know too much about Santa for him not to be real. "There's his workshop at the North Pole, Mrs. Claus, the elves, the reindeer, and his sleigh. And what about all the pictures that have been taken of him in his red suit? I've seen them. He's everywhere." I paused only long enough to take a short breath before continuing. "... on Christmas cards, in store windows, in books and magazines. And how about those radio news reports on Christmas Eve of sightings of him on his way from the North Pole. No one could possibly make all that stuff up."

I was still adamantly justifying my faith in Santa when Skippy left to throw snowballs at Billy Dean's younger brother. I called after him, "I don't believe in the Tooth Fairy though," but he was already next door compacting wet snow into fist-sized projectiles. I wanted him to know that I was not so gullible that I believed everything people told me. People could say anything they wanted to. That doesn't mean it would be true. And it doesn't mean I'd believe it. I wanted to tell him that anyone could make up pretend characters who did all kinds of magical things. It'd be easy.

Especially if you didn't have to make up all that other stuff to go along with them. You wouldn't have to figure out where they lived, or if they were married, what clothes they wore, or how they got around. Of course, you wouldn't leave them milk and cookies either, because they wouldn't be real.

But I wouldn't, however, have wanted Skippy to know that I myself had spent time daydreaming and conjuring up possible make-believe beings. I envisioned an entire cast of fairy-like elves who, like the Tooth Fairy, would possess magical powers and be capable of undetected flight. I'd even make up fairies for grown-ups. It wouldn't be for teeth, but for things that adults lose.

The Hair Fairy, I imagined, would flaunt long, flowing cascades of thick, golden hair. She would float into the bedrooms of men who were going bald and check for strands of unattached hair on their pillows. Of course, they wouldn't get money for each hair that fell out. She would simply show up every few months, make a visual assessment, and leave what she felt was appropriate compensation. Bald men like Mr. Shnair would be the richest men in the world. A smooth, shiny head would be a sign of great wealth.

I'd also have a Glasses Fairy for grandparents who were always losing their reading glasses. The Glasses Fairy, wearing a nightgown and, of course, glasses, would come and read to grandparents after they were asleep. The grandparents wouldn't know she was there, but they'd have dreams as the stories were being read. Then the Glasses Fairy would leave a little something for them. It wouldn't be money, but when the grandparents woke up the next morning, they'd find a nice pair of reading glasses under their pillow and say, "Oh, that's where I left them."

It would also be handy to have a Dust Fairy who would appear in kids' rooms every week or so to tidy up a little. It would save Moms the trouble of having to remind kids to do it. She'd arrive on a broom just like a witch, but she'd actually use the broom to sweep up. Of course, the first clue you'd have that she was only make-believe would be that your room would not actually get cleaned, and you'd still have to do it yourself. It was fun to daydream about this stuff, but in the end, that's all it was—foolish, childhood fantasies.

I blame Skippy McClay for planting the first seeds of doubt about the existence of Santa Claus. He had put a tiny crack in the foundation of my belief system that gradually grew until it could not be ignored. The more I thought about how easy it was to conceive fictitious beings, the less sure I was that Santa wasn't one of them. For the next year or so I tried to convince myself that I had not been duped— that everything I knew about Santa was, in fact, plausible. By the third grade, however, I had reluctantly concluded that I had been the victim of an elaborately executed deception. Hoodwinked. Bamboozled. But it was a glorious deception and I would not have wanted it otherwise.

As myths go, there's still no comparison between Santa

Claus and the Tooth Fairy. For my money, the most sophisticated, cunningly delusive hoax the world has ever known—the gold standard of make-believe—has to be the fat man in the red suit. And I fell for it, hook, line, and sinker.

Gullibility can be a beautiful thing.

Printed in the United States
By Bookmasters